teens
@ the library
series

101+ Teen
Programs
that work

RoseMary
Honnold

Neal-Schuman Publishers, Inc.

New York   London

Don't miss the companion Web site that accompanies this book! See preface for details!

Published by Neal-Schuman Publishers, Inc.
100 Varick Street
New York, NY 10013

Library of Congress Cataloging-in-Publication Data

Honnold, RoseMary, 1954–
   101+ teen programs that work / RoseMary Honnold.
      p. cm. — (Teens@the library series)
   Includes bibliographical references and index.
   ISBN 1-55570-453-0 (alk. paper)
   1. Young adults libraries—Activity programs—United States. 2. Libraries and teenagers—United States. 3. Teenagers—Books and reading—United States.
I. Title: 101 + teen programs that work. II. Title: One hundred and one plus teen programs that work. III. Title. IV. Series.

Z718.5 .H65 2002
027.62'6—dc21
                                                        2002029385

Contents

Figure List   xi
Series Editor Foreword by Joel Shoemaker   xv
Preface   xvii
Acknowledgments   xxi

Introduction by Patrick Jones   1

1. Make a Case for Teen Programming at Your Library   7
Overview   7
    What does Programming do for Teens?   7
    What does Programming do for the Library?   10
    How can Your Library Afford to do Programming?   11
Resources   12

2. Planning Programs   13
Overview   13
What Programs will Work in Your Library?   14
Finding Program Ideas   19
    A Dewey Brainstorm   19
    A Calendar of Ideas   19
    Coshocton Public Library's Year of YA Programs   19
When is the Best Time for a Program?   23
    The Bottom Line   23
    The Collection Connection   24
Teen Feedback   24
Resources   24

3. Summer Reading Programs   25
Overview   25
The Basic Summer Reading Program   25
A Collection of Summer Reading Independent Program Themes   28
    Circus Theme   28
    International Theme   32

Space Theme   34
History/Medieval Theme   36
Commemorative Occasions Theme   38
    The Bottom Line   38
    The Collection Connection   38
Resources   38

4. **Independent Programs and Contests**   41
Overview   41
A Collection of Independent Programs   42
Matching Games   42
    Unmask the Celebrities   42
        Variations 43
    It's a Love Match   43
        Variations 43
    Songs Inspired by Literature   44
    Misheard Lyrics   44
    Play to Win   44
        Variations 45
    What's so Great About Her?   45
        Variations 45
Trivia Games   45
    Holiday Trivia Quiz   45
    Turkey Test   46
    Sports Team Trivia   46
    Library Trivia   46
    TV Trivia and Other Trivia Games 46
Guessing Games   47
    Back To School Countdown   47
        Variations 47
    I Spy   47
    Body In The Book Drop   48
Giveaway Drawings   48
    Countdown To Christmas Comics Giveaway 48
        Variations 48
Book-Related Games   48
Word Games   49
    Thesaurically Speaking   49
    Say What?   49
    WDIM? (What Does It Mean?)   50
    Word Scrambles   50

Word Trivia 50
Cryptograms, Crosswords, and Other Games 50
Poetry Board 50
Virtual Makeover Day 51
Contests 51
Photography 52
Posters 52
Poetry 52
Essay 52
Bookmarks 52
The Bottom Line 52
The Collection Connection 53
Resources 53

5. Craft Programs 55
Overview 55
A Collection of Craft Programs 55
Beads! Beads! Beads! 56
Materials Needed 58
The Bottom Line 58
The Collection Connection 58
Mehndi Tattoo and a Taste of India 58
Materials Needed 60
The Taste of India Meal 61
The Bottom Line 62
The Collection Connection 62
Sand Art and Sand Painting 62
Materials Needed 63
The Bottom Line 63
The Collection Connection 64
Tie Dye 64
Materials Needed 64
The Bottom Line 66
Soaps and Lotions/Aromatherapy 66
Materials Needed 66
Procedures 66
The Collection Connection 67
The Bottom Line 67
More Craft Program Ideas 68
Candle Making 68
Candy Making 68

Scrap Book Picture Frames   69
Make a Journal   70
Mardi Gras Masks   71
Teen Feedback   71
Resources   71

6. Game Programs   **73**
Overview   73
A Collection of Game Programs   73
Role-Playing Games   73
Purchased Mystery Games   75
Live Clue   75
The Bottom Line   81
The Collection Connection   81
Game Show Programs   82
Survive Jeopardy and Feel Like a Millionaire   82
Whose Line Is It Anyway?   88
Board Games   89
Monopoly® Tournament   89
The Bottom Line   90
Board Game Nights, Chess, Scrabble®   91
The Bottom Line   91
The Collection Connection   91
Teen Feedback   91
Resources   92

7. Coffeehouse Programs   **93**
Overview   93
A Collection of Coffeehouse Programs   93
Poetry Night   93
Group Poetry Games   98
Music Revue/Karaoke   99
Open Mike Night   102
The Bottom Line   102
The Collection Connection   102
Teen Feedback   102
Resources   103

8. Scavenger Hunts   **105**
Overview   105
A Collection of Scavenger Hunts   106

We Have a Mission! A Space Theme Scavenger Hunt 106
Library Survivor 112
Library Tour 118
Independent Scavenger Hunts 118
    The Bottom Line 119
    The Collection Connection 119
Resources 119

9. Lock-Ins and Holiday Parties **121**
Overview 121
A Basic Lock-In Plan 121
    Medieval Theme 122
    Space Theme 122
    Beach Party Theme 123
        Games, Crafts, and Activities for a Beach Party 124
        Food for a Beach Party 126
        Prizes for a Beach Party 126
More Party and Lock-In Activities 126
    Pizza Taste-Off 126
    Fun Party Food Ideas 128
    Christmas Carry-In Dinner 128
        Anthropology Game: In the Year 20001 129
    Halloween Decorating Party 130
        The Mummy Wrap 130
    Human Bingo 132
        Variations 133
    Mad Libs 133
    Dictionary 133
    Sardines 133
    Sweet Heart Chat 134
    Twenty Questions 134
    Play-Doh Sculptionary 134
    Name That Tune 134
        The Bottom Line 134
        The Collection Connection 135
Teen Feedback 135
Resources 136

10. Programs for Teens and Parents **137**
Overview 137
    Science Fair Help Day 137

Details to Complete the Program   143
Ideas for Presenters   143
Instructions for Mad Scientist Lab Experiments   143
The Bottom Line   146
The Collection Connection   146
College Knowledge   146
The Bottom Line   148
The Collection Connection   149
International Game Night   149
The Bottom Line   149
Teen Feedback   150
Resources   150

11. Programs for Teens and Children   **151**
Overview   151
Reader's Theater   151
The Bottom Line   153
Medieval Festival   153
Carnival   156
The Bottom Line   156
Teen Feedback   156
Resources   156

12. Field Trips   **157**
Overview   157
The Borders Shopping Trip   157
Other Field Trip Ideas   160
The Bottom Line   160
Teen Feedback   160

13. Teen Volunteer Programs   **163**
Overview   163
Volunteer Jobs for Teens   164
Tips for Creating Good Volunteers   165
Rewards for Volunteers   166
How To Organize a Teen Advisory Board   166

14. Publicity   **169**
Overview   169
E-Mail List   169
Newsletters   170

Display Case   173
Schools   174
Word of Mouth   175
Media   175
Community Events   175
Resources   177

15. Record Keeping   **179**
Overview   179
Program Records   179
Evaluations   180
Circulation Statistics   181
Is it All About Numbers?   181

A Final Word   **183**
Index to 101+ Programs   185
Index   187
About the Author   195

Figure List

2–1 Teen Read Week Survey   16

2–2 Teen Advisory Board Program Poll   17

2–3 A Dewey Brainstorm of Program Ideas   20

2–4 A Calendar of Program Ideas   21

2–5 Scheduled Coshocton Public Library Teen Programs 2002   23

3–1 Summer Reading Program Survey   27

3–2 Circus Theme Book Ratings   29

3–3 Circus Theme Puzzles   30

3–4 Under the Big Top Game Poster   31

3–5 International Theme Book Ratings   32

3–6 International Theme Puzzles   33

3–7 Space Theme Book Ratings   34

3–8 Space Theme Puzzles   35

3–9 Medieval/Fantasy Theme Book Ratings   36

3–10 Medieval/Fantasy Puzzles   37

5–1 Bead Program Publicity Display   56

5–2 Bead Program   57

5–3 Mehndi Instructions Handout   59

5–4 Mehndi Program   60

5–5 Chicken Curry Meal   61

5–6 Tie Dye Instructions   65

5–7 Tie Dye Washing Instructions   65

6–1 Warhammer Role Players   74

6–2 Dungeons and Dragons Role Players   75

6–3 Live Clue Notebooks   78

6–4 Jester Crime Scene   79

6–5 Live Clue Team   80

6–6 Survive Jeopardy and Feel Like a Millionaire Program   82

6–7 Couch Potato TV Trivia Questions   83

6–8 Take Time to Read Library/Book Trivia Questions   84

6–9 Get Ready to Rumble Sports Trivia Questions   84

6–10 Want Fries With That? Fast Food Trivia Questions   85

6–11 Two Thumbs Up Movie Trivia Questions   85

6–12 Trick or Treat Halloween Trivia Questions   86

6–13 Name That Tune Music Trivia Questions   87

6–14 Let's Make a Date   89

6–15 Monopoly® Tournament   90

7–1 Poetry Night Table   94

7–2 Poetry Night Teen Poets   95

7–3 Poetry Night Name That Poet Poster   96

7–4 Poetry Night Name That Poet Answer Sheet   97

7–5 Music Revue Guest Musician   100

7–6 Music Revue Karaoke   101

7–7 Music Revue Closing Song   101

8–1 We Have a Mission Team   111

8–2 We Have a Mission Team   111

8–3 Library Survivor Program   117

8–4 Library Survivor Program   117

9–1 Beach Party Floor Plan   123

9–2 Beach Party Room   124

9–3 Beach Blanket Bingo Card   125

9–4 Pizza Taste-Off Ballot   127

9–5 The Mummy Wrap   131

9–6 Human Bingo Card   132

10–1 Science Fair Help Day Presenter   138

10–2 Science Fair Help Day Presenter   139

10–3 Science Fair Help Day Kitchen Chemist   140

10–4 Science Fair Help Day Mad Scientist Lab   142

10–5 College Site-Seeing Tour Page 1   147

10–6 College Site-Seeing Tour Page 2   148

11–1 Reader's Theater Cast   153

11–2 Medieval Fair Hair Wrapping   154

11–3 Medieval Fair Fishing in the Moat   155

12–1 Borders Shopping Trip Permission Slip   158

12–2 Borders Shopping Trip   159

13–1 Teen Volunteers   164

13–2 Teen Volunteers   165

13–3 Teen Advisory Board Application   168

14–1 E-Mail Sign Up   170

14–2 Newsletter Article List   172

14–3 Newsletter Title List   172

14–4 Photo Release   173

14–5 Display Case   174

14–6 The Book Tree   176

15–1 Program Record   180

Series Editor Foreword

Joel Shoemaker

We know that libraries and teens are a good fit.

Teens are good for libraries because many of them have grown accustomed to outstanding library services as children. In libraries with a children's department, kids are used to being served by specially trained staff, reading from specialized children's collections, with other support services and special programming, in a unique, "child-friendly" section of the facility. We know that teens will soon enough become the parents, voters, school board, and library board members who will, among other things, make important decisions that help decide the fate of our libraries. We are committed to the idea that the world will become a better place if these young people have access to the best, most current and accurate information and ideas. We know they also need and want the most interesting, wide-ranging, and challenging recreational reading that they can get.

Teens belong in libraries. But perhaps, like me, you have heard a young adult librarian ask:

- "How can I get more teens into our library?"
- "Teens come in here all the time. What can I do with them?"
- "I want to do a program about (fill in the blank). Has anyone ever done something like this? Can you tell me what works and what things to watch out for?"

Have you been wanting to start a teen advisory board but been unsure how to start? Or do you have a teen advisory board already, and are looking for ways to expand their horizons?

We know that one of the most important things we can do for teens is to answer their often deeply felt but unvoiced query, "Am I the only one . . . ?" YA librarians can identify with that, especially working in smaller libraries, often in smaller cities and towns where they are likely the only staff member charged with providing YA services. Most frequently, they also have other library responsibilities, too. How can such a librarian provide the best programs for teens in their part-time environment and on a limited budget? The author has been there, and she'll show you how to do that.

Like all the books in the *teens @ the library* series, *101+ Teen Programs That Work*

- draws from the best, most current research,
- targets the changing needs of today's teenagers,
- cites the most innovative models,
- provides practical suggestions that have been real-world tested, and
- calls on each of us to realize the highest ideals of our profession.

There is no need, however, to re-invent the wheel. *101+ Teen Programs That Work* is replete with examples of real teen-tested answers to these questions and more. And more importantly, it is based not so much on gimmicks as it is on the positive, can-do, teen-centered approach to YA librarianship to which we all aspire. While RoseMary Honnold's examples are practical, they are also based on building skills that make teens more capable and that contribute to their personal growth. Participation in library-sponsored programs of the type advocated by Honnold provide young people with more than a sense of community. They can be important steps toward helping teens build a real community, based on sharing, cooperation, knowledge, and skill. Her suggestions may inspire you, too, to advocate for the creation of a teen advisory board, or a full-time YA staff position in your library. And you, like the author, may find that you are the perfect person for the job.

Public librarians most often think in terms of programs—"What can I have these teenagers do?" School librarians are more accustomed to dealing with curriculum—what is being taught. But it does not have to be an either/or proposition. Public librarians help teens learn, and school librarians provide activities, motivating promotional programs, workshops, and author visits, to name a few, for their students. Honnold's book provides plenty of examples of programs and activities that can work equally well in either of these library settings. All teachers know that learning for many teens is enhanced by physical activity, or by active participation. Many of the programs outlined here can be adapted to become great teaching tools for a multitude of library purposes. The bottom line in this case is not dollars, but experiences that help teen library users grow into more successful, competent people.

These sample programs are based on experience with real teens. They reveal a wonderful sense of humor, show a broad-ranging creativity, provide insight into both the kinds of library information kids need and the kinds of activities teens enjoy, and all are packaged with strategies to ensure that your efforts will be successful. For a perspective as fun and energetic as teens themselves can be, I recommend to you this outstanding book.

Preface

The libraries of the twenty-first century are no longer mere depositories of print material. Libraries are vibrant meeting points—centers of useful information technology and community activities—offering programs that will educate and entertain their faithful patrons and attract new ones. Library journals and professional young adult resources tell us that teens comprise 25 percent of our patron mix.

Good teen programs often attract the young adults of the community to the library to see what other services are available. Programs also give librarians an opportunity to interact with, educate, and entertain teens, while providing positive role models and experiences. The role of today's young adult librarian is to provide programming that will bring teens into the library and keep them coming back. Small libraries have the special challenge of achieving this on a small budget and with limited staff time.

101+ Teen Programs That Work is a how-to program guide for librarians that work with teens in a public or school library setting. Many program ideas are presented and many individual programs are mapped out step-by-step as examples. All of these programs are possible on a limited budget with limited staff time. And teens actually like them—they are field-tested!

ORGANIZATION

Chapter 1, "Make a Case for Teen Programming at Your Library," offers the reasons your library should design programs for teens and how those programs will benefit the teens of your community and your library. "The Forty Developmental Assets for Adolescents" developed by The Search Institute gives us a firm foundation for building our own positive philosophy towards teen programming.

Chapter 2, "Planning Programs," describes how to figure out what programs will work in your library, includes survey samples, and offers lists of possible topics and activities to consider for programs. The methods presented to gain teen input will help you spend your time and the library's money wisely on programs the teens will enjoy. A sample year of programming at my own library illustrates the concept of having something happening for teens every month of the year.

The third chapter, "Summer Reading Programs," is a great place to start teen programming. The basic independent program is complemented with monthly social programs that are described more fully in subsequent chapters. Several themes are described, and examples of book rating slips and puzzles for the themes will spark your imagination when designing your own summer reading program.

Less occasion-specific programs are offered in Chapter 4, "Independent Programs and Contests," with suggestions for variations, suitable to adapt to almost any topic or time. The independent programs are quick and easy and give YA librarians recovery time between social events, while keeping the teens involved.

Chapter 5, "Craft Programs," describes successful art-related programs that have worked for teens in our library. Out of necessity, a restricted budget is kept in mind as well as limited creativity (for those of you that believe you have none). From beads, sand painting, and soap making to mehndi and tie dye, these crafts will give the teens something cool to take home that they have created themselves.

The sixth chapter covers "Game Programs." Some of our most enjoyable and successful programs have revolved around games. Role-playing, game shows, and board game tournaments are fun social occasions for teens and the adults lucky enough to help.

"Coffeehouse Programs" are the subject of Chapter 7, which features tips on transforming your meeting room into a coffeehouse. Poetry nights, music revues, and open mike nights are included with group games to do with the teens.

Chapter 8, "Scavenger Hunts," is another crowd-pleaser. My own interpretation of having fun while learning is most fully realized in the scavenger hunts we stage at our library. Detailed explanations of two of the hunts will inspire you and your teens to create even more. An example of a hunt that can be used during a classroom tour is also included.

Lock-ins and holiday parties are covered in Chapter 9. Many games and activities are described and tips for having a successful party or lock-in are included. A Pizza Taste-Off, a Christmas Carry-In Dinner, and a Beach Party will show teens what a cool place the library can be. You will also find a few recipes for treats the teens can make themselves at the parties.

Chapter 10, "Programs for Teens and Parents," describes family-oriented programs. The Science Fair Help Day program is exemplified in detail with instructions for putting together a Mad Scientist Lab. College Knowledge showcases library resources for future college students and the International Game Night is an example of a just-for-fun program for the whole family.

Teens can have a great time entertaining young children by helping with large children's programs or by presenting a reader's theater skit. Chapter 11, "Programs for Teens and Children," tells of some of these events you'll want to try with your teens.

An activity our Teen Advisory Board looks forward to every year is our Borders Shopping Trip. The teens choose books for the YA collection and bookplates are placed in the books to show who chose them. The twelfth chapter, "Field Trips," tells how to pull off a trip such as the Borders Shopping Trip and what to take. There is a sample permission slip to have parents sign.

Chapter 13, "Teen Volunteer Programs," will guide you in forming successful volunteer programs and teen advisory boards. Lists of jobs that teens can do, suggestions for making the process go smoothly, and ideas for rewards for their work are included.

As we near the end of the book, Chapter 14, "Publicity," covers this essential element for all of these programs. Getting the word out to teens can be tricky since the traditional media may not work for this age group. E-mail lists, newsletters, photo shoots, display cases, and community events are alternatives suggested in this chapter.

The book ends with the short Chapter 15, "Record Keeping." You will learn what records to keep, why keep them, and how to use them to help your cause, and a sample program record form is provided.

Throughout *101+ Teen Programs That Work* you will find photos, suggestions for making the Collection Connection, costs of the programs when applicable, lists of resources, and one of my favorite things, feedback from the teens that have participated in our programs. Since many resources are found online, I have created a companion Web page at *See YA Around* that will keep the online resources up to date. The address is

www.cplrmh.com/teenprograms.html

If you have trouble connecting to any of the sites listed in this book, check this site for updates.

BACKGROUND

My public library has housed all the ideas in this book. Coshocton Public Library's young adult program is now nearly seven years old. It began when our staff heard C. Allen Nichols speak at a library in-service about serving teens. He inspired four of us on the staff to use our "spare time" to have a summer reading program for teens and to start a teen advisory board. I was further encouraged when I attended the Kent State YA Symposium and heard Patrick Jones speak for the first time. His enthusiasm is contagious and I went back to our library filled with ideas but not enough time to implement them! After a couple of years of great responses from the teens for the limited programming we offered, we decided to suggest the library needed a full-time YA librarian. Our very supportive director agreed and I was lucky enough to capture the position.

My duties include all YA programming, ordering all YA materials, putting up displays, and decorating in the YA room. I also work at the reference desk 16 hours a week, so, like many of you in smaller libraries, I am wearing several hats! *101+ Teen Programs That Work* will help you to have at least one teen independent or social program per month all through the year even if your schedule is hectic like mine.

Thinking up programs for teens is the exciting and creative part of my job. Planning with the teens is fun and seeing the happy faces of teens laughing and having a good time is rewarding. Some of the teens I have worked with since they were seventh graders all through high school on the Teen Advisory Board. It has been a pleasure watching them mature and make a contribution with their volunteer work at the library. We have had a few adventures and many laughs together and I am happy to get to include some of their thoughts in this book.

If you have a YA program and need new ideas or are just starting out in young adult services, this is the book for you. If you need convincing that teen programming is the right thing to do, start at the first chapter. After that, you can read it from cover to cover, browse for programs that catch your interest in the table of contents, or look for ideas on what to do for an event, season, or topic in the index. Keep it near your desk for easy reference when you are wondering what your next program will be. The many programs included will keep your teens busy for years to come!

Acknowledgments

The team at Neal-Schuman Publishers: Charles Harmon, Michael Kelley, and Gary Albert who patiently worked with this new author through the writing and publication of this book.

Patrick Jones for suggesting I write this book, and his faith that I could do it.

Ann Miller, director of the Coshocton Public Library, who has given me support and room to explore what I can do in YA services in our library and beyond.

Cathy Haynes, Holli Rainwater, and Mike Ontko, my co-workers who started our first Teen Advisory Board with me in our "spare time" and Connie Surdyk, who has since joined the team.

My office mates, Sara Mesaros, Pam Williams, Ron Martin, and Kris Ringwalt, who tolerate fumes from science experiments gone amuck, work around strange structures such as book trees and mounds of props for scavenger hunts, and help eat up the leftover snacks, all in good humor.

Sandy Marvin, Coshocton High School librarian, who shared her program ideas and experiences in a school library environment.

Jayne Honnold, Chillicothe High School English teacher (and my sister-in-law), who shared her ideas and experiences in a classroom environment. Constance Coker, a great friend, who not only has been very supportive, but has brainstormed with me and shared her amazing creative ideas.

My family . . . my daughters and their husbands for sharing talents, ideas, and resources, and my husband for keeping the home fires burning during the writing of this book.

Introduction

Patrick Jones
author of *Connecting Young Adults and Libraries*

In 1998, the American Library Association (ALA) teamed with DeWitt
Wallace–Reader's Digest Fund to investigate what was going on in public libraries regarding programming for youth. The ALA sent a survey
out to 1,500 public libraries in the United States. All 461 public libraries
that serve populations of 100,000 or more received the questionnaire. Libraries serving 5,000 to 100,000 were sampled if they met certain criteria
regarding staff, hours open, and annual operating expenditures.

The results were a good news/bad news thing. The major findings of the
survey were presented in the publication *Programs for School-Age Youth in Public Libraries.* The good news is that of the 1,256 libraries that returned the
questionnaire, all but eight indicated they offered programs for school-age
youth. The programming that is taking place in most of these libraries is directly related to the tried and true activities related to motivating reading
and providing entertainment/cultural opportunities.

Now, the bad news: the majority of programs are geared to elementary,
then middle school students, with the fewest programs designed for high
school–age youth. And the worst news is, despite all the research telling librarians the value of youth participation, the role of youth in planning and
implementing programs is minimal. Where libraries reported some responsibilities for youth, the most common response was "set up" or "clean up"
for reading programs or "recruit youth to participate" in community-service
programs. The youth involvement seemed more concerned with benefiting
the library than the youth. So while there was youth involvement, there wasn't
an engagement of youth that built their development assets

The development assets concept is a framework developed by The Search
Institute (www.search-institute.org) based on solid research. This framework
identifies 40 critical factors for young people's growth and development.
When drawn together, the assets offer a set of benchmarks for positive ado-

lescent development. The assets clearly show important roles that families, schools, congregations, neighborhoods, youth organizations, and others in communities play in shaping young people's lives—and libraries.

These 40 developmental assets represent everyday wisdom about positive experiences and characteristics for young people. The assets can be divided into two large groupings: external assets and internal assets. The external assets focus on positive experiences that young people receive from the people and institutions in their lives. Four categories of external assets are included in the framework:

- *Support:* Young people need to experience support, care, and love from their families, neighbors, and many others. They need organizations and institutions that provide positive, supportive environments.
- *Empowerment:* Young people need to be valued by their community and have opportunities to contribute to others. For this to occur, they must be safe and feel secure.
- *Boundaries and expectations:* Young people need to know what is expected of them and whether activities and behaviors are "in bounds" and "out of bounds."
- *Constructive use of time:* Young people need constructive, enriching opportunities for growth through creative activities, youth programs, congregational involvement, and quality time at home.

The second set of 20 assets are internal assets. They focus on the internal qualities that guide choices and create a sense of centeredness, purpose, and focus. Indeed, shaping internal dispositions that encourage wise, responsible, and compassionate judgments is particularly important in a society that prizes individualism. The four categories of internal assets are:

- *Commitment to learning:* Young people need to develop a lifelong commitment to education and learning.

- *Positive values:* Youth need to develop strong values that guide their choices.

- *Social competencies:* Young people need skills and competencies that equip them to make positive choices, to build relationships, and to succeed in life.

- *Positive identity:* Young people need a strong sense of their own power, purpose, worth, and promise.

All the research collected and analyzed by The Search Institute points to one conclusion: **the more assets young people have, the more likely they are to become caring, competent adults, and the less likely they are to engage in**

dangerous or at-risk behavior. Assets are powerful influences on adolescent behavior—both protecting young people from many different problem behaviors and promoting positive attitudes and behaviors. This power is evident across all cultural and socioeconomic groups of youth.

So, here is another good news/bad news thing. The research and the youth development movement have people thinking about assets and providing clear guidance on what works. But the research also shows that too few young people experience enough of these assets. The average young person surveyed experiences only 18 of the 40 assets. Overall, 62 percent of young people surveyed experience fewer than 20 of the assets. Thus, most young people in the United States do not have in their lives many of the basic building blocks of healthy development. For libraries, the news is even worse as one of the least reported assets is "reading for pleasure" with only 24 percent of teens surveyed by The Search Institute report reading three or more hours a week. Also low on the list is attendance at youth programs with only 59 percent of teens reporting spending any time in an organized activity.

So why does this matter and what to do with it? Well, it is another good news and bad news thing. The good news is that the ALA survey on youth programs was followed by the report *Public Libraries as Partners in Youth Development: Challenges and Opportunities.* In this report, the Dewitt Wallace Fund describes how it used these survey findings plus other research to create an initiative that seeks to increase the availability of high-quality programs for school-age youth in public libraries, especially in low-income communities. Putting its money where its mouth/words were, Dewitt Wallace awarded ten urban public libraries huge grants to take the findings and turn them into reality. The Public Libraries as Partners in Youth Development project, developed with Urban Libraries Council, has resulted in innovation in young adult programming for urban libraries.

This leads us to our final good news/bad news pair. The bad news is that all of the money and attention went to large urban libraries. Good for them and other big libraries, but most public libraries are not big, are not urban, and do not serve large numbers of low-income youth. While there is a connection between low income and "at-risk" behavior, the youth development research also indicates that all youth need to build assets to ensure they do not engage in at-risk behavior. Thus, all youth are at-risk of becoming "at-risk." While teens in smaller towns may not face the same challenges as urban youth, they also normally lack access to a broad network of social services and youth agencies. In many smaller towns, other than school and a few clubs, the public library is the only place that can provide programs that build assets. So, how do medium-sized and small libraries develop successful programs for teenagers?

They read *101+ Teen Programs That Work.*

This is not good news, this is great news. In the pages that follow, RoseMary lays out the case for young adult programming, outlines the planning process, and then provides step by step "how I did it good and you can too" instructions on all sorts of programs that engage youth. There is ample information on how to promote programs, how to involve youth, and even how to measure program success.

Yes, we need to continue to count the number of teens who attend programs, but we also need to focus on the outcomes. Write down how many people walked in the door, but be just as concerned about what happens to them after they walk out the door. We need to care about numbers, but one of the keys to successful teen programs is to focus on the quality of the experience as opposed to the quantity of attendance. In a sense, the main number that matters is always the same: 40. How did the program build the 40 developmental assets? How did the library contribute to healthy youth development? How did the library thus contribute to making the community better? Those are hard questions, but as funders become more interested in outcomes, it is one that libraries—of all sizes—need to think about.

As you read this book, as you "borrow" program ideas, or as the book inspires you to work with youth to develop your own programs, keep the list of 40 assets by your side. When you build programs that build assets for the teens in the community and for the library, then it is one of those good news/ good news things.

RESOURCES

American Library Association. 1999. "Reports Explore Potential of Public Libraries to Serve Development Needs of Youth" [Online]. Available: www.ala.org/news/ v4n20/reportsexplore.html [2002, June 26].

Benson, Peter. 1998. *What Teens Need To Succeed: Proven, Practical Ways To Shape Your Own Future.* Minneapolis: Free Spirit Press.

Challenges and Opportunities: Public Libraries as Partners in Youth Development. 1999. New York: Dewitt Wallace-Reader's Digest Fund.

Jones, Patrick. 2001. "Why We Are Kids' Best Assets." *School Library Journal* 47, no. 11: 25–28.

Programs for School-Age Youth in Public Libraries: Report of a Survey Conducted for the Dewitt Wallace-Reader's Digest Fund. 1999. Chicago: American Library Association.

Roehlkepartain, Jolene L. 1997. *Building Assets Together: 135 Group Activities for Helping Youth Succeed.* Minneapolis: Search Institute.

Search Institute. 2002. "Development Assets: An Overview" [Online]. Available: www.search-institute.org/assets/ [2002, June 26].

Search Institute. 2002. "Percentages of 6th- to 12th-Grade Youth Experiencing Each Asset" [Online]. Available: www.search-institute.org/research/assets/assetfreqs.html [2002, June 26].

Urban Library Council. 2001. "Public Libraries as Partners in Youth Development" [Online]. Available: www.urbanlibraries.org/youth.html [2002, June 26].

Young Adult Library Services Association and Patrick Jones. 2002. *New Directions in Library Service to Young Adults*. Chicago: ALA Editions.

Young Adult Library Services Association Professional Development Center. 2002. "Professional Development Topics: Programming" [Online]. Available: www.ala.org/yalsa/profdev/programming.html [2002, June 26].

Chapter 1

Make a Case for Teen Programming at Your Library

OVERVIEW

Whether you are a veteran or a new young adult librarian, you may find yourself in the position of convincing management or reminding yourself that programming for teens is worthwhile. Developing a positive philosophy about serving teens arms you as an advocate for teen activities and teen collection development in your library. Many libraries have one person serving teens and only in a part-time capacity. Justifying the time and energy spent on developing a program and asking for assistance and funding may be your first task. Having a philosophy in mind can serve to make a case for teen programming in your library to the management and also is a reminder that you are making an important contribution to the lives of the teens in your community. When asked why you should provide a program, your answer should explain what the program does for teens and what it does for the library. This chapter may help you reinforce your own philosophy or help you develop one so you are a prepared and effective advocate for teens, helping your library develop a warm welcoming attitude towards teens.

What does Programming do for Teens?

The Search Institute, a not-for-profit, independent organization, whose mission is to advance the well-being of children and teens, has compiled a list of 40 assets that help young people grow into caring responsible adults. The results of their research conclude that the more of these assets the teens have, the more likely they will engage in positive behavior and resist negative behaviors. As a young adult librarian in a public or school library, you are in the position to provide opportunities to help the teens in your community develop many of these assets by organizing a Teen Advisory Board and providing good teen programming. The 40 assets are categorized into eight different types listed below, each followed with ways you and your library programming can help fulfill them. The first four are the external assets and the last four are the internal assets. More can be learned about The Search Institute by visiting their Web site, listed in the resources at the end of this chapter.

- *Support*: The librarian who interacts with teens regularly with a positive attitude can provide a supportive adult relationship for them outside of their families. Working with teens on a craft or at a Teen Advisory Board (TAB) meeting allows them to see you as a positive role model and helps develop a comfortable relationship that will extend to everyday library interactions. The teens will view the library as part of a caring community when space, materials, and programs suited to their needs and interests are provided as a result of their suggestions, and a staff member is particularly interested in their library experiences and seems approachable.
- *Empowerment*: The changes in your library collection and service resulting from the teens' suggestions show them they are valued in the library and the community. They see their opinions are heard and their ideas are implemented and they feel empowered. A program offered, a book purchased, a game played, and furniture purchased all as a result of suggestions made to you through surveys or conversations tell a teen you are listening and value his opinion. Teens perform a useful service to the library and to other teens when volunteering to help plan and implement programming that will appeal to other teens and assist with library work.
- *Boundaries and Expectations*: Clear guidelines and fair consequences for behavior in TAB meetings and social programs teach fair and equal justice, mutual respect, and acceptable social behavior. Teens learn responsibility when deadlines need to be met when planning and publicizing a program or publishing a newsletter.
- *Constructive Use of Time*: Brainstorming TAB meetings, craft programs, volunteering, and book talks are examples of a few creative and productive ways teens can spend their time at the library. Social interaction is valuable in a teen's life and the library can provide an organized and supervised setting for safe, interesting, and fun social activities. Independent programs give teens a chance to participate in an activity when their schedules get tight and their time in the library is limited. Creative expression in music, art, poetry, and writing can find a home

in a library. A combination of independent and social programs presents a variety of teaching styles, making learning opportunities available to different kinds of students. Teens will benefit from learning from you, learning from each other, and learning on their own.

- *Commitment to Learning:* Reading is the ticket to the world of knowledge. Encouraging reading, learning, and use of the library are a library program's main purposes. Programs can coincide with school assignments and enhance homework skills. Contests and games that encourage library use to find answers help develop good research skills the teens will be able to apply to schoolwork. Programs should always have an element of fun and entertainment so reading and learning and being at the library is a pleasurable experience. A clear connection between the program and the library's collection will encourage teens to explore new ideas and develop new skills after the program is over.
- *Positive Values:* Teens are learning that caring about others is an enjoyable and rewarding activity when they have opportunities to volunteer to help with senior and children's programming and plan programming for other teens. Sharing responsibilities, learning each other's strengths, and appreciating one another's contributions to the group build their respect for each other and in turn their self-respect.
- *Social Competencies:* When teens help plan, support, and attend programs, they are learning skills that will help them in their adult social lives. How to plan a gathering, how to make a list of priorities and details, how to make the gathering purposeful and relevant, and how to be responsible for their share in the implementation of the program are all part of learning to work with others and being responsible in honoring commitments. They can see the reward in following through with their responsibilities when a program goes well and is attended by their friends. They experience positive social interactions with other teens and with adults helping with the programs.
- *Positive Identity:* When teens have a say about what their place in the library will be and what kinds of programs they need or want, they learn that their ideas and suggestions are important. They serve a purpose in helping provide good service to their fellow teens in the community. When they complete a program, they can feel proud in what they have learned and accomplished, as a participant or as a planner. Skills learned in the library through independent and social programs will be useful to the teens throughout their lives. Many programs that encourage planning for the future and teach them to care for their minds and bodies help teens develop a strong sense of self.

Your supportive role is important to help teens in your community develop these assets and to help them find constructive use of their free time. The library's financial and time investment in the teens is an investment in the future. We can help teens become more capable, comfortable, and responsible people ready to take a productive place in our communities and in society. When teens fall short of our high expectations, it is helpful to remember that they are people under construction. They need our guidance to get them through the construction zone.

What does Programming do for the Library?

Your library becomes an important community center when it provides educational and entertaining programs for all ages, including teens, securing its position in the community for the future. If any programs are provided to the public in your library, then teens should be included as part of the public. The library sets a good example for the community by valuing teens when there is a special collection and programs developed just for them. A mutual respect develops between the library staff and the community's teens when they feel heard and recognized. For many libraries, this may mean an improved after-school atmosphere with teens involved in an organized productive activity or engaged in friendlier interactions with the library staff.

Children's librarians offer programs regularly to bring in youngsters to develop an early habit of using the library. Developing YA programming that will attract teens continues the habit to foster lifelong library use. The library attracts new patrons, who may not be avid readers, with interesting programs that offer visual, aural, and active learning opportunities. These patrons will then learn of the many audio/visual materials and special needs materials available to them at the library and find reading materials they may have not imagined were available in a library. Expanding services to reluctant and nonreaders widens the support for the library in the community.

Teens will begin to consider librarianship to be an interesting and exciting career choice. The librarian is no longer someone who sits behind a desk shushing them, but is someone who cares about their interests, is willing to try new ideas, and is able to have fun. Relationships are established through the interaction involved in the programs and the planning. It is very satisfying for a teen to choose librarianship as a career because of their experiences in your library. Mamie Alsdurf, a Coshocton Teen Advisory Board member, is planning a career as a librarian. In her own words, "I am a wanna be librarian and being able to not only enjoy the library as a place of resource, but also to get involved in fun activities with other teens definitely makes my appreciation of public libraries stronger. YA activities are definite necessities." These active teens not only become lifelong library users, but will contribute to the profession as adults.

How can Your Library Afford to do Programming?

If you are convinced you should offer programs to teens but are short of staff or funds, you have the special challenge of thinking out of the box and making every program dollar and planning minute count. You will need to use your resources wisely and creatively. All of my programs are inexpensive or nearly free, depending upon what I have on hand to use at the time. None of them require an expensive guest to present the program if you are willing to do some research and experimenting yourself. Involving friends and relatives with interesting hobbies or talents, using materials on hand, using the Internet, recycling and collecting materials from others for crafts and displays, and putting your teens to work are keys to having something going on every month for teens at your library on a limited budget. You may also learn how to do a few new things along the way while spending time interacting with the students as you teach them how to do new crafts, improve library skills, and play games.

Independent programs are less expensive to put together than social programs. Craft programs that use recycled materials save money and volunteers for social programs can save staff expense. Prizes and food are usually the major expenses in the programs in this book.

Local fast food restaurants will often donate free food coupons for prizes. Theaters, gyms, music, book, and comics stores may be sources for free donations or gift certificates. Co-workers and friends may have the craft supplies you need tucked away in a closet and will be glad to find someone who can use them. If your library has a Friends group, approach them for funds for teen programs and the teens can return the favor by helping at book sales.

Our library has a membership with Naeir, a company that redistributes manufactured goods to nonprofit organizations. A membership fee and shipping is all you pay and you can get an amazing assortment of party supplies, prizes, display items, and decorations. Whatever is available in the catalog often inspires ideas for programs and displays. Other inexpensive sources are Big Lots stores, Warehouse Clubs, and The Flower Factory, to name a few. Shopping online can often lead you to a good bargain when you are looking for a specific item. For an example, when shopping for mehndi kits, I was able to read about what I needed, read about how to do mehndi tattooing, comparison shop for kits, and order the kits all in the same afternoon online. Other inexpensive resources for incentives and prizes are The Oriental Trading Company, U. S. Toy, and Smilemakers, who specialize in small inexpensive toys and prizes. Also, there aren't too many teens that wouldn't be happy winning a six-pack of Mountain Dew!

Collaborating with another organization in your community that supports teens is a possibility if you do not have the space or staff to help you for some of these programs that require a gathering of teens. If there is a coffee-house in your community, there is no need to create one. Contact the owner to arrange a poetry night that will bring teens together for a program and benefit a local business as well. A sports demonstration may be better suited in a gym, yet be sponsored by the library. Connecting with the places where teens hang out in your community increases your ability to publicize an activity to an interested crowd.

Food is an important element in teen social activities. Many experienced teen workers say "If you feed them, they will come!" Food can also be a major expense. You and your Teen Advisory Board can save money by asking area businesses for donations for special programs. Donated pizza for a Pizza Taste-Off or free-food coupons from fast food restaurants are excellent incentives and prizes teens will love. Staff members or teens who like to bake may donate to your activity. Buying snacks and soda on sale and from discount stores can help stretch the food budget. Soda is less expensive in two-liter bottles, but you will need to buy cups, while soda cans are recyclable and may be a source for funds to buy more soda. Popcorn is an inexpensive alternative to chips and when freshly popped, smells inviting to a crowd of teens.

RESOURCES

Carnegie Corporation of New York. 1992. *A Matter of Time: Risk and Opportunity in the Nonschool Hours.* New York: Carnegie Corporation.

Jones, Patrick. 1998. *Connecting Young Adults and Libraries, 2nd ed.* New York: Neal-Schuman Publishers, Inc.

Jones, Patrick. 2001. "Why We Are Kids' Best Assets." *School Library Journal* (November): 44–47.

Naeir.org [Online]. Available: www.naeir.org/ [2002, May 10].
> Note: Our membership dues are $575.00 a year and we pay up to $200.00 shipping for each shipment. For approximately $1500.00 total for 2001, we received over $10,000.00 in products, including prizes and incentives for all departments, decorative and display items, party supplies, craft supplies, office supplies, and many other miscellaneous items.

The Oriental Trading Company [Online]. Available: www.oriental.com/home.html [2002, May 10].

The Search Institute. 2000. *Forty Developmental Assets for Adolescents* [Online]. Available: www.search-institute.org/assets/forty.htm [2002, May 10].

Smilemakers [Online]. Available: www.smilemakers.com/ [2002, May 10].

U. S. Toy [Online]. Available: www.ustoy.com [2002, May 10].

Chapter 2

Planning Programs

OVERVIEW

Isaac Asimov wrote in his autobiographies that he was often asked where he got all his ideas for his stories. His reply was "I just make them up!" Few of us are lucky enough to have his imagination but we can develop a talent at thinking creatively when it comes to making the most of limited resources and letting our imaginations roam free. Successful programs begin with a glimpse of an idea. It requires a certain state of alertness and openness when opportunities and ideas happen by, and an ability to file the information away for use when it is needed.

In my office you would find a large file drawer of programming information. Some are developed programs I have used and some are files of ideas under different topics waiting for the right time or opportunity to use them. You would also find a lot of books for reference and also a few strange articles waiting for a moment of inspiration for a future program. A box of acrylic prisms sat on my shelf for almost two years until I was putting together a bead program. I recalled hearing about beaded prisms at a Renaissance Festival and added them to the bead program supplies and they were very easy and popular projects. What materials do you have around? Cardboard picture frame holders might become a scrapbook picture frame project, rolls of Kraft paper might become table covers for doodling or wall covering to draw murals. The next time someone offers you an odd collection, just say yes and save it for some future brilliant program idea.

Maybe you have tried a program that sounded like a good idea but it didn't work. Either teens didn't come or the ones that showed up didn't get into it and you are left wondering what went wrong. If you got the program idea from another library and it had worked for them, it may seem like you did something wrong. If you will take into consideration the demographics of the teens in your area and the community activities already in place when planning your program, you will have a better chance of attracting your teen audience. This chapter is about where to find ideas for programs and which ones will work in your library for your teens. Using these methods will help you spend your time and the library's programming budget wisely on programs that your teens will enjoy.

WHAT PROGRAMS WILL WORK IN YOUR LIBRARY?

We start with what librarians do best: research! In the business world this research is called direct marketing and it means you must first identify the needs and wants of the teen audience you want to attract. The target audience for the young adult department in my library is grades 7–12, since the children's department does programming and collection development for up to 6th grade. The first step is to ask the potential audience what they need and want. Teens are the best resource for finding out what your library can do for them. Don't waste time and money producing a program you think is a great idea but find out too late teens won't come to it. Involving teens in the planning stages will help you provide what the teens need and want in a way that they will enjoy.

There are a few different methods of direct marketing teens that give useful results. The first is a suggestion box. This is the simplest, easiest, and cheapest way to get honest feedback from the teens already in your library. You may choose to make a suggestion box a permanent presence in the YA area. A form with a few questions will get the answers you need if you are wanting to find out about a specific program or collection ideas. If the suggestion box is going to be a permanent fixture, change the questions periodically to rekindle interest and provide a continuing source of information for improvements to your service.

Here is a sampling of questions you may want to ask:

- Which nights or days of the week are the best for you to attend an activity at the library?
- Would you attend a craft program at the library? If so, what craft would you like to learn?
- Who are your favorite authors? (music groups?) (actors?)
- What is your favorite way to learn something new? Do you like to read how to do it, have someone show you, or do it yourself?

You can also direct market teens with paper or e-mail surveys. These are usually more thorough and may ask a few demographic questions, so you may gain a better picture of your audience. The surveys can ask about past or future programs, collection development, or even decorating and furniture suggestions for the YA area. I use surveys two times a year. The Summer Reading Survey is about collection development and the YA area and the Teen Read Week Survey is always about programming. The surveys are made available in the YA room. The summer surveys are turned in at the Summer Reading Program drawing box and the Teen Read Week surveys are turned in at the reference desk.

The first survey shown in Figure 2–1 was used as a Teen Read Week promotion. When the teens turned in the survey at the reference desk, they received a flyer about the TRW program, a coupon for $1.00 off fines, and a candy treat. A survey of this type is helpful to see if the program publicity you have been using is working and if the programs offered in the past year were interesting to the teens. There was a chance for some positive interaction between librarians and teens when the surveys were turned in. The results showed me that the publicity I was doing wasn't reaching all the teens that were interested in the programs I was offering.

When our library first started thinking about expanding the YA programming we offered, a few of us had a brainstorming session to generate a list of possible programming ideas. We presented this list as a poll to the teens at a board meeting to determine what kinds of programming would interest them. The most popular results gave us an idea where to start. See Figure 2–2.

A clipboard interview is also fun to do with teens. While adults may want to avoid them in the malls, teens enjoy giving their opinions and will be pleasantly surprised when you ask them what they think about anything in the library. You can ask a few of the survey or suggestion box questions or ask for collection ideas such as: Who are your three favorite musical groups? You can use this information to not only add music to the collection but also to develop an independent program about music and a display to feature books and music. You can do this survey with the teens already in your library or ask permission to conduct the survey at school during lunch.

Your Teen Advisory Board can brainstorm with you. I rely heavily on our TAB, not only as an idea resource, but also for feedback about my ideas as well as planning and implementing the programs. Teen Advisory Board meetings are programs in themselves. They take planning and preparation and food, but are well worth the effort. The feedback and assistance from the teens are essential in developing a successful program and the personal relationships are rewarding.

You can network with other YA librarians for programming ideas. A whole world of young adult librarians are at your fingertips through several listservs. Meetings with other YA librarians in our region through the Mid Ohio

Grades 7–12 only!
Help us plan the programs you would like to see at the Coshocton Public Library!
Turn this survey in at the reference desk or to RoseMary and see what a treat
it is to visit the library!

Age _____ Gender _____ Grade _____ School _____

Did you attend any of the following programs this past year?

Please rate them according to how you enjoyed them if you were there.

1 is first rate   2 is just okay   3 is don't bother having this again

Name of program:	Check if attended:	Rating (circle):
Pizza Taste Off and Game Show Oct 2000	____	1 2 3
College Knowledge Nov 2000	____	1 2 3
Turkey Test Trivia Game Nov 2000	____	1 2 3
Countdown to Christmas Comics Giveaway Dec 2000	____	1 2 3
Science Fair Help Day Jan 2001	____	1 2 3
Just Another Love Song Match Game Feb 2001	____	1 2 3
Teen Poetry Night Apr 2001	____	1 2 3
Mehndi Tattoo and a Taste of India Jun 2001	____	1 2 3
Where in the World Are You Reading Summer Reading Program	____	1 2 3
Monopoly Tournament July 2001	____	1 2 3
Library Survivor and Beach Party Lock In Aug 2001	____	1 2 3

If you didn't come to any of these programs, tell us why:

What kind of programs do you think teens would like to see happen at the library?

Have you thought about serving on the Teen Advisory Board? Why or why not?

Thank you for taking the time to fill out this survey!

Figure 2–1 Teen Read Week Survey.
**This program survey will show you if your publicity is working and
the programs you are offering are of interest to the teens in your library.**

Please rate the following in terms of how interested you are in the programs or services that the library could offer to young adults:

I=Interested V=Very Interested N=Not Interested

____ 1. Having a homework helper on the main floor to help kids in the afternoons and early evenings with their school assignments.

____ 2. Hosting a coffeehouse where teens could come for entertainment.

____ 3. Having a poetry reading where teens could read their original poetry.

____ 4. Publishing a book of teens' original poetry.

____ 5. Having a study space/homework center in the large meeting room a few days a week.

____ 6. Having a Current Assignments section in the library where students could go and find materials to help with their latest assignments.

____ 7. Science Fair Workshop

____ 8. Babysitting Workshop

____ 9. Substance Abuse Workshop

____ 10. Job-seeking Workshop

____ 11. Bulletin Board with Summer Job postings

____ 12. Back to school style show

____ 13. Photography workshop

____ 14. Hobbies/collections workshop

____ 15. Dream interpretation workshop

____ 16. Camping/hiking/survival skills workshop

____ 17. Chess tournament

____ 18. Scrabble tournament

____ 19. Origami workshop

____ 20. Baseball card swap

____ 21. Nintendo/computer game swap

____ 22. Research paper workshop

____ 23. Peer tutoring

____ 24. Creating a YA web page

____ 25. Teen Jeopardy

____ 26. T-shirt painting workshop

____ 27. Earth Day/recycling

____ 28. YA newsletter

____ 29. Student liaison at schools

____ 30. Collect and post school newspapers in the library

____ 31. Calligraphy workshop

____ 32. Joint activities with Museum Teen Board

____ 33. Have a YA board dinner

____ 34. Make the YA area more comfortable

(How?) _____

Figure 2–2 Teen Advisory Board Program Poll.
A program poll given to your Teen Advisory Board will give you a list of program ideas your teens would like to help participate in and plan.

Library Organization's (MOLO) YA Special Interest Group has been very helpful to me, as well as attending workshops and chapter and state conferences that feature YA program and service ideas by other YA librarians. Developing a presentation for a workshop or conference is a very valuable learning experience. The research can lead you to many new resources for ideas to use in your own library.

Research the teen culture by reading popular teen magazines, watching MTV, and reading professional young adult literature to find more ideas of what you can do to enhance your teens' library experiences. Know who is popular in music, TV, movies, and what styles and fads are current. This knowledge can help you design your program and develop the YA collection. One of our MOLO meetings was spent discussing the trends found in teen magazines. Each of us read a teen magazine assigned to us at the previous meeting. We shared the fads, trends, news, and commented on the content and focus of each of the magazines for the rest of the group. We came away with a better idea of which new magazines the teens in our own libraries would like and a broader knowledge of current fashions and trends.

Find out what your community is already offering teens. With your limited time and space and funds, there is no reason to repeat what someone else is doing. Try to fill in the areas the community doesn't offer. Consider cooperating with another organization to put together a program. They may have the contacts, you may have the meeting room, or vice versa. Contact your local high schools' librarians and find out what is happening in their libraries. You may be able to coordinate a program with an assignment or coordinate tours or classroom visits with special research assignments.

If a program idea sparks your interest, make a note of it, even if it doesn't seem workable at the moment. Collect program ideas and where you heard them or read about them in a file so when you need to put one together, much of your research is done. Think of this file as your program bank and invest in it regularly. If paper files are too cumbersome, keep a file of floppy disks. When a good idea comes up in an e-mail or on a Web site, copy and paste it into a WordPad file and save it on a disk. You may have one that says "lock in ideas," "sports program ideas," or "poetry ideas." When it comes time to plan a program, you will have lots of ideas stored and ready to present to your TAB or to work with yourself.

Finally, if you find a program that your teens enjoy, keep it going. Ask them to tell you what they liked and how it can be improved for the next time. The teens will begin looking forward to that event and you have a program that just needs a few finishing touches every year.

FINDING PROGRAM IDEAS

A Dewey Brainstorm

Patrick Jones has used an exercise in his workshops that produces a list of program topics generated by his audience. The exercise involves going through the Dewey Decimal system and thinking of topics and ideas for programs. This process doesn't require a fleshed-out program as a result, but is meant to help us start thinking of the many topics available to us on our shelves that we can build programs around. Figure 2–3 is a compilation of ideas I have collected from workshops, e-mails, books, daydreaming, and TAB meetings.

A Calendar of Ideas

The American Library Association has designated special weeks of the year to celebrate reading, books, and libraries. Holidays, commemorative occasions, special events, and seasons are also inspiration for programs. Browsing through a calendar of events may suggest when you can best implement a particular program.

Coshocton Public Library's Year of YA Programs

This is a sample list of teen programs for a whole year at our library. A few of these are annual requested favorites, such as the Poetry Coffeehouse, Monopoly Tournament, and the August Lock-In. I recently added craft programs and plan to do two craft programs a year and incorporate a craft or two in the lock-in. For the months we are not having social programs, I have an independent program in the YA room. This gives me a little break and some planning time for the next social program while keeping teens interested in what is happening at the library. Our TAB meets once a month too, which I consider to be a social program.

WHEN IS THE BEST TIME FOR A PROGRAM?

After-school programs need to be scheduled around sports and band practices, homework, and dinner. An hour or two after school works at our library for TAB meetings and craft programs. TAB meetings are the last Monday of each month. Thursday evenings for social gatherings like the coffeehouses and game shows or Saturday mornings for longer programs like the Monopoly Tournament work well also. Lock-ins are held on a Friday night in August when the library closes early and before the fall school sports schedule begins. When scheduling evening programs for teens, keep in mind sports, music competitions, and practices to avoid as many conflicts as possible. In

Dewey #	Program Ideas
000	computer and Internet classes, build a Web site, Internet scavenger hunt, trivia scavenger hunt, e-mail pen pals between TABs, library tours
100	ghost story telling, astrology signs, X-Files trivia, dream analysis
200	mythology gods and goddesses matching game, multicultural holiday celebrations, Xena and Hercules trivia
300	college preparation workshops, social issues workshop, mehndi tattooing, etiquette workshop, recycling program, mummy wrap, fashion show, fairy tale reader's theater, holiday parties, holiday crafts, pen pal clubs, fan mail clubs, Halloween make up
400	sign language, hieroglyphic cartouche craft, spelling bees, Scrabble tournaments, cryptograms, Dictionary games, jargon, lingo, acronyms
500	science fair day, astronomy programs, insect collections, birds, fish, animals, math puzzles
600	cooking workshops, chocolate parties, makeovers and skin care, getting your first job, pet shows, gardening workshops, babysitting clinics, Lego competitions, car model shows, car repair, paper, brand names, airplanes, bicycle and motorcycle maintenance
700	game shows, sports and athlete identifying and trivia, karaoke, crafts, collector card trade shows, TV and movie trivia, comics drawing workshops, make jewelry, comics trade show, photography contests, role playing games, music, art, yo yo contests and demos, name that tune, graffiti tables, board and card game tournaments, wrestling and martial arts demos, make puppets
800	poetry nights and contests, improv nights, acting workshops, reader's theater, writing workshops, mystery nights, battle of the books, book discussion groups, homework center, puppet shows
900	Celebrities, politicians, historical figures, international game night, multicultural crafts, celebrity games, decades trivia and theme nights, women's history trivia, famous authors, explorers, Native American crafts: dream catchers, god's eyes, sand art

Figure 2–3 A Dewey Brainstorm of Program Ideas.
Keep and add to a list of program ideas in all the categories in the Dewey Decimal system. When you need a program on a topic or theme, an idea is there waiting for you.

Month	Program Occasions and Ideas
January	New Year's Day- write a resolution to enter a drawing, Inauguration Day- trivia quiz about the new President and his family, Martin Luther King's birthday- trivia quiz about Martin Luther King, National Radio Month- match pop hits with musicians, vote for favorite station, National Hobby Month- origami or paper airplane craft available in YA room.
February	Presidents' Day- match names of children or pets or state where they were born with the Presidents, Valentine's Day- match up couples, match love songs with singers, Black History Month- match photos and names with accomplishments, American Heart Month- exercise program, health program, Chinese New Year- Chinese horoscopes, Chinese cooking lesson, Haiku contest, Leap Year- trivia quiz, Leap Year party, Mardi Gras- make Mardi Gras masks, Winter Olympics- Read for the Gold, vote for coolest winter sport event.
March	Spring- equinox trivia, weather records, Women's History Month- match famous women with their achievements, National Craft Month- craft program, Saint Patrick's Day- limerick contest, Irish authors, Passover- Jewish authors, match famous Jews and their achievements, Easter- make bookmarks for children's room, Easter trivia quiz.
April	April Fool's Day- write a joke for a drawing entry, post the jokes. Arbor Day- tree facts, plant a tree on library property, Baseball Season- match team logos with teams, card swap, Tax time- first job workshop, Keep America Beautiful Month- recycling program, National Poetry Month- Poetry coffeehouse, poetry contest, Zoo and Aquarium Month- match colorful tropical fish with their names, National Child Abuse Prevention Month- babysitting clinic, National Library Week- match author photos with book covers, library trivia, Stump the Librarian Contest, Prom- fashion show, makeup workshop.
May	Election Day- mock election, unmask politicians, Cinco de Mayo- taco party, Kentucky Derby- Derby trivia, horse trivia, horse stories and series, Asian Pacific Heritage Month- island hop scavenger hunt, luau, May Day, Mother's Day, National Bike Month- bike anatomy test, Older Americans Month- Reader's theater for seniors, Memorial Day- in memory of bulletin board, Graduation- job interviews, writing resumes.

Figure 2–4 A Calendar of Program Ideas.
Compile a list of all library events, holidays, and seasonal program ideas
through the year. These are all opportunities for programs for teens.

Month	Program Occasions and Ideas
June	Summer- Reading Program, Father's Day, Gay and Lesbian Book Month, Flag Day, Dairy Month- Got Milk? Cookie trivia quiz, summer sports, National Rose Month- match pictures of roses with their literary names.
July	National Parks and Recreation Month- match the national park with the state, Independence Day- vote for contemporary patriots, National Hot Dog Month- hot dog trivia quiz, cookout, National Ice Cream Month- ice cream trivia quiz, make your own sundae.
August	National Inventors Month- match an inventor with an invention, Romance Awareness Month- romance mad libs, Home Business Month- jobs for teens workshop, Back to School- countdown drawing.
September	Autumn- football, Labor Day, Library Card Sign Up Month, Baby Safety Month- baby sitting clinic, Self Improvement Month- yoga or other exercise/meditation program, Hispanic Heritage Month, National Grandparents Day- Reader's theatre, fix a meal for grandparents, photos with grandparents, Rosh Hashanah, Yom Kippur- Jewish authors games.
October	Domestic Violence Awareness Month, Homecoming- fashion show, makeovers, Columbus Day, Teen Read Week- game show programs, surveys, coffeehouses, Computer Learning Month- computer training, Consumer Information Month- match business logos with favorite teen brands, Halloween- decorate for children's parties, mummy wrap game.
November	Election Day- mock election, Children's Book Week- fairy tale reader's theater, Veteran's Day, Native American Indian Heritage Month- bead crafts, sand art, Child Safety and Protection Month, International Creative Child and Adult Month- craft program, USA Thanksgiving- Turkey trivia, National Author's Day- writing workshop, make a journal.
December	Winter- basket ball, wrestling, Chanukah, Christmas, Kwanzaa- holiday parties and trivia games, Universal Human Rights Month, Safe Toys and Gifts Month, Food for Fines.

Figure 2–4 A Calendar of Program Ideas (*continued*)

January	Science Fair Help Day, TAB meeting, publish YA Today
February	Make a Tie Dye Valentine, TAB meeting
March	Borders Shopping Trip for TAB, TAB meeting, publish YA Today
April	Teen Poetry Night Coffeehouse, TAB meeting
May	Reader's Theatre Production for Dogwood Arts Festival, Free Comic Book Day, Summer Reading Program Promotion, TAB meeting, publish YA Today
June	Summer Reading Independent Program, Soaps and Lotions Craft Program, TAB meeting
July	Summer Reading Independent Program, Monopoly Tournament, TAB meeting, publish YA Today
August	Lock In, Back to School Countdown, TAB meeting
September	College Knowledge, TAB meeting, publish YA Today
October	Teen Read Week survey, TRW Program, TAB meeting (decorate for Children's parties)
November	After School Craft, TAB meeting (wrap homebound gifts), publish YA Today
December	Countdown to Christmas Comics Giveaway, TAB meeting (Christmas Party)

Figure 2–5 Scheduled Coshocton Public Library Teen Programs 2002.
This is a sample year of planned teen programs at Coshocton Public Library. More programs may be added if a new idea comes along that fits in my budget and schedule.

many communities, Wednesday night is considered to be church night. Consult school calendars and teens in the TAB or in your library when scheduling social programs.

THE BOTTOM LINE

Sadly, the cost of a program is one of the most important factors for many libraries. In The Bottom Line section of each program chapter in this book, I will share the approximate costs of the programs and how to cut expenses. If you use as many free and available items as you can, costs will depend upon what you have on hand. When you need additional adult help, volunteers are free, however, I feel it is a better thing when the teens and library staff get to interact on a more personal level to develop better relations between the library and teens.

THE COLLECTION CONNECTION

Always promote your collection and services at your programs with displays, commercial breaks, or library materials placed around the room and on tables. This will inform your teens of what the library has to offer for further knowledge about the topic, validates the program for your director, and hopefully increases circulation. In each of the following chapters, there is a list of possible subject area connections you can make with your collection for the programs. Use these collections for displays, commercial breaks, and creating booklists for handouts.

TEEN FEEDBACK

Several teens who have attended the programs at our library were asked to write a sentence or two about what they thought of them. I have included these quotes so you have a bit of the teens' point of view about the types of programs in each chapter.

RESOURCES

The books, journal articles, and Internet resources I found helpful when planning these programs will be listed in the Resources sections of each chapter. These lists will be places to go for more information, resources for program development, and resources for materials for some programs.

Honnold, RoseMary. 2000. *The Who, What, Why, Where, and How of Managing a Teen Advisory Board* [Online]. Available: www.cplrmh.com/tab.html [2002, January 20].
Teen Advisory Groups – Advisory Discussion (TAGAD-L). A discussion forum for the advisors of any public library teen advisory group. To subscribe, e-mail tagad-l-subscribe@topica.com.
YA-YAAC - YALSA's listserv for teen advisory group advisors. To subscribe, e-mail listproc@ala.org with no subject line. In the body type: Subscribe YA-YAAC your first name your last name.

Chapter 3

Summer Reading Programs

OVERVIEW

Establishing a Summer Reading Program for teens is a good place to start teen programming as your library will most likely have one in place for children. You have a ready audience as the young teens that have just moved out of the children's program will be looking for something to do the next summer. In our library, the YA summer reading program is intended for grades 7–12, however many 5th and 6th graders have already migrated to the young adult area, so they are allowed to enter, too.

Summer is often the only time teens can find the time to read for fun and need to be encouraged to do so. Otherwise their memories of libraries will be picking up books they had to read for school with little pleasure connected to the act of reading or visiting the library. Displays are important during the summer to attract the teens to the special recreational collections intended just for them.

THE BASIC SUMMER READING PROGRAM

The basic independent summer program is easy to set up and maintain. The Summer Reading Program remains in place for June and July so teens may come and participate independently at their leisure. The purpose is to encourage reading and to make returning to the library throughout the summer an enjoyable activity. Book rating forms are available for entries in weekly drawings for prizes. The prizes may be whatever you can afford to give away, such as: candy bars, books, comics, movie passes, or free food coupons. Winning a prize in a drawing is fun and exciting no matter what the prize is, but the more exciting, useful, or fun the prize is, the more incentive there is to enter the drawing. The more books they read, the more book rating entries they can fill out for more chances on the prizes. The book ratings follow the library's theme for the summer and are intentionally a little humorous.

The bulletin board or poster and drawing box should coordinate to advertise the theme and the program. Covering the bulletin board and drawing box with wrapping paper with a design that follows the theme is an easy and fast way to do this or use poster board and add borders and party confetti that complement the theme. Post the dates of the drawings and the first name and last initial of who won the prizes each week. If you need pictures to show the theme, search the Internet for photos you can download and print. Be shameless in promoting your first teen program by using huge arrows, lots of color, foot prints on the floor, signs by the front door—anything that will catch the teens' attention to let them know there is something new for them to do.

In addition to the book rating forms, you can add a different puzzle or quest to the entries each week that can be made to fit your theme using a puzzle making program online. Crosswords, word searches, mazes, and a variety of other word puzzles are available to be customized to the theme. Variations of trivia games are also popular; we have used Cleveland Indians trivia questions from the Internet and library trivia questions that were made up about our library and staff. The puzzles could be about your services or collection to promote library use and are encouraging for teens who aren't heavy readers, because they can enter at least once a week with a puzzle or trivia answer while practicing their library skills. One of the weekly puzzles during the program is an annual questionnaire survey about the YA collection. I use the information from the survey for collection development.

One of the weekly activities can be a simple paper craft that can be displayed in the YA room for the duration of the program. The teens will have helped decorate their space with their creations. A summer reading record decorated with clip art that matches the summer's theme is a nice keepsake for teens. A list that says "What I Read the Summer of 2002" will be interesting and amusing to them in a few years.

In our library's Summer Reading Program, the teens may read books, comics, magazines, and listen to audio books, using any library materials for the program. The program is to encourage library use as well as reading for fun. The rating forms ask for an opinion, rather than being a test of knowledge, to make the program as unschool-like as possible. The book rating forms can be displayed for other teens to see and/or tallied to see what the most read items were that summer. The results make a good follow-up display to summer reading. Display the books or scan the fronts and make a banner that says "I Know What You Read Last Summer." Add a bookmark with all the most popular titles.

Where in the World are YOU Reading?

The Coshocton Public Library is interested in providing you with the very
best reading materials for middle and high school students.
To do that, we need your feedback.

AGE: SCHOOL: GRADE:
MALE FEMALE (circle one)

Circle your answers:
1. What are you reading this summer?
    Magazines   Newspapers   Books   Comic books
    Other _____
2. Where is your favorite place to read this summer?
    _____

3. In fiction, what kind do you like best:
    Adventure Historical Fantasy Horror Humor Mystery/Suspense
    Romance Science Fiction Sports Teen problems Graphic novels
    Classics Other: _____
    Favorite author: _____
4. In nonfiction, what do you like best:
    Health History Music TV Movies Biographies Poetry
    True crime   Sports   Science   Other: _____
    Favorite Subject _____
5. How do you find out about new books?
    Friends' suggestions Browsing in store   Browsing in library   Librarians
    Teacher   Television   Amazon.com   Reviews/ads   New book lists
6. Do you use the YA music collection?   Yes   No
7. Are there CDs you would like to see added to the collection?
    _____

8. If you could do one thing to improve the selection of reading and
    listening materials for teenagers at the Coshocton Public Library, what
    would it be?

Additional comments:

Place in Drawing Box and THANK YOU!!!
Summer Reading Program 2001
Coshocton Public Library

This survey is anonymous, please fill out a pink slip for weekly drawing!

Figure 3–1 Summer Reading Program Survey.
This survey will give you feedback about the YA collection.

A more recent development has been summer reading programs online. If you have a teen Web site already, you can add an online registration, book review or rating forms, polls, quizzes, trivia games, or Internet scavenger hunts. Sites such as Quia.com offer a space to build your own online game site to fit the theme using their game generator. You can also add booklists and links to the site. Customized polls can be made at Pollcaster.com. These fun additions increase traffic to your Web site where you should also be featuring library materials and promoting social programs to tempt the teens to come in and visit the library.

Along with the independent prize drawings, social programs give teens a chance to gather together for fun (and maybe educational) events at the library during the summer. I plan three summer social programs, one each month. Two of these have become traditions that the teens look forward to every year: The Monopoly Tournament and The Lock-In. The third program is usually designed around the library's SRP theme. For example, during the international SRP, I offered the Mehndi Tattoo and Taste of India program. These programs give the teens a chance to socialize, have fun, and find out what is available at the library and it gives me a chance to interact with and get to know the teens.

All adults, teens, and children that have participated in summer reading at our library are invited to a pool party at our community pool at the end of July sponsored by the Friends of the Library. The party is held after public hours and door prizes are awarded every fifteen minutes. Tickets are available the last weeks of the program.

A COLLECTION OF SUMMER READING
INDEPENDENT PROGRAM THEMES

The following samples of book rating forms and puzzle ideas have been used at our library with successful results. The same basic plan works with any theme. These can be created as soon as you decide on a theme. Our library has followed the State of Ohio Library's theme for several years. I try to work with the same theme as the children's and adult departments so all the displays and publicity coordinate for the library. A state or regional theme or individual library themes can be adapted to suit teens.

Circus Theme

For the summer reading theme, "Your Library: The Greatest Show in Town," our library used a circus theme. The bulletin board is divided into three rings: one ring to promote the monthly program, one to present the weekly puzzle, and one to show the previous week's answer and winners. The clown faces the teens create for one week's activity decorate the room throughout the program.

The Library:
The Greatest Show In Town
Summer Reading Program
Rating Form

Title_____

Circle One:
*Feed it to the lions!
**A dog and pony show!
***Boss clown!
****Ringmaster!

Name _____
Phone_____

Place form in the Summer Reading box for weekly prize drawings!

Figure 3–2 Circus Theme Book Ratings.
The teens submit one form per item read into weekly drawings for prizes.

Who's Clowning Around? (Identify photos)	Create poster of celebrity photos. Disguise with clown noses and costumes. Teen identifies the celebrities. Reveal full photos the following week.
Intermission (match food pictures with food trivia)	Create poster of circus/carnival food pictures. Print food trivia on colored paper and cut into balloon shapes. Teens match picture with trivia. Post answers the following week.
Under The Big Top (multiple choice circus trivia)	Print circus trivia questions on tent shapes and attach the top edges of the tents to poster. List answers to questions under the tents. Teens lift the big top to see answers.
Amazing Treats (maze)	Candy Maze at Puzzlemaker. Post solution the following week.
Circus Lingo	Post a list of circus lingo words. Teens create definitions of the words. Post the correct definition and most creative/funny definitions submitted by the teens.
Send In the Clowns	Provide white and brightly colored paper, markers, scissors, glue and masking tape. Teens create clown faces to decorate the YA room during summer reading.
It's Showtime	Post lists of most popular YA titles according to the book rating forms. Provide forms for teens to find the authors/call numbers of three of the titles.
Teen Collection Survey	Collection development survey. Use the results to see what you need to add to the collection and what the teens like that you already have.

Figure 3–3 Circus Theme Puzzles.
The puzzles give teens a chance to use their library skills.

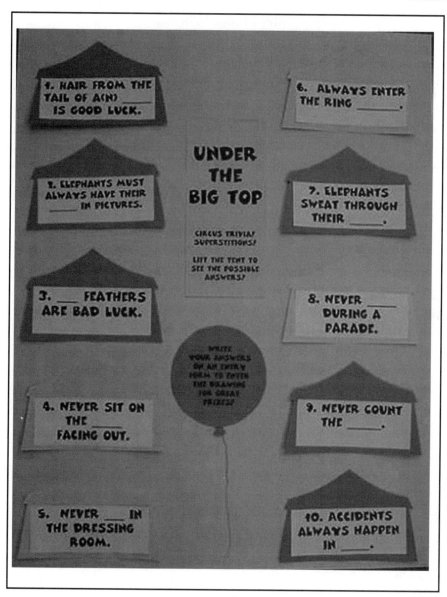

Figure 3–4 Under the Big Top Game Poster.
Games may also be presented on posters. Under the Big Top is a circus trivia quiz. The teens look under the tents to find the multiple choice answers. An answer form will go into the weekly prize drawing.

International Theme

"Where in the World Are You Reading?" was an international/travel/vacation summer reading theme. The bulletin board and drawing box for this International theme were decorated to look like packages that had been shipped all over the world. Kraft paper, twine, postcards and international stamp images downloaded from the Internet, and a FRAGILE stamp were quite effective embellishments. One section of the "package" featured the weekly puzzle and the past week's solution, another section was reserved for promoting that month's social program and the last promoted the book ratings and prize drawings. International flags (from Naeir) hung from the ceiling and travel posters collected from local travel agencies decorated the walls. Books on foreign languages, foreign countries, and multi-cultural fiction were on display on every horizontal surface. Prizes were CD cases for the guys and Caboodles for the girls (all from Naeir)—both are items you might take on a trip.

Where In the World Are You Reading?

Summer Reading Program
Rating Form

Title_____

Circle One:
*Hand me an airsickness bag!
**This book goes nowhere!
***Nice place to visit (but I wouldn't want to live there)
****First class all the way!

Name _____

Phone_____

Place form in the Summer Reading box for weekly prize drawings!

Figure 3–5 International Theme Book Ratings.
The rating forms show you what the teens are reading and what they like.

Nothing to do This Saturday?	Create a cryptogram at Puzzlemaker that is promoting a social program. Post the solution the following week as publicity for the program.
Where in the World are You Reading?	Create a crossword puzzle at Puzzlemaker. Capital cities are clues, states are the answers. Post the solved puzzle the following week.
Ohio's Rivers (use your state)	Create a word search at Puzzlemaker with the names of 16 Ohio rivers. Post the solution the following week.
Tutankhamun	Print out the King Tut maze from Puzzlemaker. Print the solution to post the following week.
Taking a Trip?	Create a tile puzzle from Puzzlemaker. Post the solution the following week. (This puzzle was a tribute to Douglas Adams. The solution was "Don't forget to take The Hitchhiker's Guide to the Galaxy!")
Take a Plane!	Provide paper and patterns for paper airplanes. Display paper airplane books. MSPublisher has airplane templates with instructions. Provide a small entry slip for the weekly drawing.
Take Me Out to the Ball Game	A logic puzzle with a grid for figuring out what color shirt a father and his sons wore to a ball game, what they ate, and their names. Logic puzzles can be found in books and on the Internet.
Teen Collection Survey	Collection development survey. Use the results to see what you need to add to the collection and what the teens like that you already have.

Figure 3–6 International Theme Puzzles.
The puzzles give reluctant readers a chance to win in the prize drawings.

Space Theme

"Out of This World and into Books" was our outer space reading theme. Wrapping paper with space ships decorated the bulletin board and drawing box. Space murals created by the TAB decorated the walls. The murals were spacescapes and fantasy space views made with a roll of dark blue paper for the base, colored paper, foil paper, and glitter glue for decorating. Photos of planets and space ships were cut out of discarded space books and added. Space, astronomy, astrology, and science fiction series and science fiction movie books were featured.

Out of This World and Into Books!

Summer Reading Program
Rating Form
Title_____
Circle One:
*Highly illogical, transport me to another book!
**Meets Starfleet regulations
***May it live long and prosper
****Moves at warp speed

Name _____

Phone_____

Place form in the Summer Reading box for weekly prize drawings!

Figure 3–7 Space Theme Book Ratings.
The humorous ratings help deliver the message that reading is fun.

Star Search	Decorate a star to hang in the YA room during the summer reading program. Provide stars cut from card stock and stickers, glitter glue, and markers for decorating. Provide small entry slips for the weekly drawing.
Who's World Is It?	Match sci fi authors with their sci fi worlds. List authors on one side of entry form, names of their worlds on the other. Post answers the following week.
Star Wars Crossword	Crossword puzzle with Star Wars characters as answers, character descriptions as clues. Create puzzle at Puzzlemaker. Post the solved puzzle the following week.
Rings Around Saturn	Create a ring shaped maze at Puzzlemaker. Post solution the following week.
Search the Solar System	Create a word search with names of planets, moons, sun, comets at Puzzlemaker. Post solution the following week.
Build a Space Ship	Offer paper and patterns to make origami Star Wars ships and Space Shuttle paper airplanes. Provide a small entry slip for the weekly drawing.
Star Trek Cryptogram	Create a cryptogram at Puzzlemaker using a famous space related quote, such as "Space, the final frontier, these are the voyages...." Post the solution the following week.
Space Trivia	Create a multiple choice trivia quiz about space. Use the Internet or astronomy books to write the questions. Post the answers the following week.
Teen Collection Survey	Collection development survey. Use the results to see what you need to add to the collection and what the teens like that you already have.

Figure 3–8 Space Theme Puzzles.
The puzzles are constructed to be completed during a library visit and may take about 15 to 20 minutes to finish.

History/Medieval Theme

"Incredible Library Time Machine" was the summer reading theme when our library decided to focus on the Medieval period. Rolls of brown Kraft paper covered the available wall space in the YA room. Crenelations were cut along the top and stone block lines drawn on the paper to create the look of castle walls. The bulletin board was covered with a red poster board, adorned with crown and scepter party decorations. The social programs and weekly puzzles were featured on the board.

Readers at the Round Table

Summer Reading Program
Rating Form

Title_____

Circle One:
*Feed it to the dragons!
**It took an act of heroism to read this!
***Some magical moments
****Fantastic!

Name _____

Phone_____

Place form in the Summer Reading box for weekly prize drawings!

Figure 3–9 Medieval/Fantasy Theme Book Ratings.
Matching the ratings with decorations and the theme pulls the independent program together.

Coat of Arms Quest	Make a coat of arms to hang in the YA room. Create with coat of arms shapes precut from card stock for the base. Provide colored paper shape and clip art to represent teen activities and interests, glue sticks and calligraphy markers for names and tape for hanging. Leave up throughout the summer reading program to help decorate the room.
Castle Questword	Crossword puzzle with castle words and clues. Create puzzle at Puzzlemaker. Post the answers the following week.
Author Quest	Famous author word search. Create at Puzzlemaker using best selling author names. Post the answer the following week.
Favorite Author Quest	Vote for favorite YA author. Create a list of popular YA authors. Post results the following week.
Magazine ReQuest	Magazine title word scramble. Make a list of YA magazines in the collection. Scramble the letters. Teens can circle their favorite title and suggest a title to add to the collection. Post a list of the most popular the following week.
King Arthur Quest	Match Arthurian characters and their roles. List the characters on one side of the entry form, their character descriptions on the other. Post the answers the following week.
Late Book Quest	Write creative excuses for returning books late. Post most creative, funniest, etc. the following week.
Teen Questionnaire	Collection development survey. Use the results to see what you need to add to the collection and what the teens like that you already have.

Figure 3–10 Medieval/Fantasy Puzzles.
The same puzzles can be changed to fit the summer's theme each year.

Commemorative Occasions Theme

Significant historical events in the community, state, or country should always be celebrated in the library, where history is saved for all to access. The teens can learn about your local heritage in a fun and entertaining way. When Ohio celebrates its bicentennial in 2003, the state summer reading theme will be structured around the bicentennial celebration. Famous Ohioans, Ohio history, Ohio authors, Ohio trivia, and Ohio tourist attractions will be featured in decorations, displays, puzzles, games, book ratings, and programs. Many resources are being created at the state government level to celebrate the bicentennial.

THE BOTTOM LINE

An independent Summer Reading Program involves very little expense except for prizes. Most of the materials are paper and bulletin board decorations, which your library already has in stock. Photos can be downloaded from the Internet and printed on regular paper or cut from discarded magazines. Spend whatever money you have on the prizes. Some libraries like to award one big prize and it is a good draw for them. My own feeling is the more prizes you have, the more teens you can make happy, as long as they are prizes teens will enjoy. The little toy prizes that please children will not please the teens! I try to collect enough prizes for six winners per week, but I would sacrifice quantity before quality. Teens can help you shop in catalogs for prizes they would like.

THE COLLECTION CONNECTION

Summer is a good time to promote your pleasure reading collections and audio/visual materials you may have. Series paperbacks, comics, software, music CDs, gaming books, magazines, and videos are all good choices to use in displays. The teens have more leisure time to enjoy them in the summer. Books that follow the library's summer reading program theme are also obvious choices. If space is a premium, just stack ten books on a table or shelf with a shelf talker or tent card that says Ten Cool Books About Space, Ten Great Books About Medieval Times, etc., or put a book face out at the end of each shelf that has to do with the theme.

RESOURCES

Couch, Ernie and Jill. 1992. *Ohio Trivia*, rev. ed. Tennessee: Rutledge Hill Press.

Discovery Schools Puzzlemaker [Online]. Available: www.puzzlemaker.com [2002, May 10].

MBK Consulting. 2002. *Links For Ohio Bicentennial: Resources for Excellent Reference Services* [Online]. Available: www.mbkcons.com/wkshp/ohio2000/ohio2000links.htm [2002, May 10].

Ohio Biography [Online]. Available: www.ohiobio.org/ [2002, May 10].

Ohio Film Commission Feature Films [Online]. Available: www.ohiofilm.com/picture/features.asp [2002, May 10].

Ohio Film Commission Ohio Celebrities [Online]. Available: www.ohiofilm.com/picture/celebs.asp [2002, May 10].

Ohio History Central [Online]. Available: www.ohiokids.org/ohc/index.html [2002, May 10].

Ohio Historical Society [Online]. Available: www.ohiohistory.org/ [2002, May 10].

Ohio Memory Online Scrapbook [Online]. Available: www.ohiomemory.org/ [2002, May 10].

OPLIN [Online]. Available: www.oplin.lib.oh.us/ [2002, May 10].

Pollcaster [Online]. Available: www.pollcaster.com [2002, july 31].

Quia [Online]. Available: www.quia.com [2002, May 10].

Simpson, Martha Seif. 1997. *Reading Programs For Young Adults: Complete Plans for 50 Theme-Related Units for Public, Middle School and High School Libraries.* Jefferson, North Carolina: McFarland & Company, Inc. This book has fun ideas for book rating forms for many reading program themes.

Zurcher, Neil. 2001. *Ohio Oddities.* Cleveland, Ohio: Gray & Company.

Chapter 4

Independent Programs and Contests

OVERVIEW

Independent programs are games that can be used throughout the year and can be adapted to many topics and themes. Like the summer reading basic program, these programs are left up for a period of time so teens may come in and participate at their leisure. Our independent programs usually last two-four weeks and are intended for grades 7–12.

Ideas for these programs can be gleaned from teen magazines, *Chase's Calendar of Events*, holiday themes, the YA collection, *VOYA*'s pop culture quizzes, and popular subject areas in your collection or pop culture themes. *The Literature Teacher's Book of Lists* is a great help when collecting titles or authors for a subject area to create a game and book display to go with it. It has many other lists that will help when creating games, such as a list of gods and goddesses and other mythological characters and creatures and famous writers on film. Independent programs are cheap, fast, and easy to put together. The prizes can be whatever you can afford or what you can get for free. They are fun and offer something special just for the teens in your library on a regular basis and can educate teens about the many resources available at the library.

Make the game colorful, include pictures, and make the instructions simple. Any pictures you need can be downloaded from the Internet, cut from discarded magazines, or collected from the vertical file. Scan book covers for book related games. Make an attractive poster or bulletin board, a drawing box and entry slips, and provide pencils. The hole in your drawing box shouldn't be big enough for hands to reach in and secure any openings with heavy tape before decorating the box. Wrapping paper can coordinate the drawing box and the bulletin board. If using a poster board, add pre-made bulletin board borders, photos, confetti, cut out letters—an attractive font if printing text—glitter glue, and stickers to jazz it up. Photos make a bigger splash when matted or framed with colored paper. Clear tape or squares of clear contact paper placed underneath the parts of a matching game will make it possible to move taped pieces to the correct positions when revealing the answers at the end of the game.

Advertise with a sign by the main entrance to your library, an article in your newsletter, school announcements, or make bookmarks or flyers for the main desk. On drawing day, choose your winners and give them a call. Post the answers and the winners' names on the bulletin board and put the prizes at the main desk for easy pick up.

Google is a good search engine when looking for trivia on the Internet. The advanced search is the quickest way to find what you want when you use phrases to narrow the search. Google also has an image search that finds photos of celebrities and other pictures quickly.

A COLLECTION OF INDEPENDENT PROGRAMS

The variety of independent programs presented here are described so you can put them together quickly and easily with materials available in your library. A few variations are suggested to illustrate how easily these programs can be adapted to different occasions and topic.

MATCHING GAMES

Matching games are fairly easy since the answers are provided. These games can be made more difficult by making them fill-in-the-blank games so the teens have to provide the answers. Both approaches require the teens to have a bit of knowledge or to do some research in the library.

Unmask the Celebrities

Make a poster with numbered photos of celebrities. Mask their eyes with black rectangles of paper. The object for the teens is to identify the celebrity. If you laminate the photos and tape the masks over the plastic, then you can pull them off at the end of the contest when you post the names under each photo. Laminating also makes the poster available for reuse at a branch library. Answer sheets should be numbered with blanks for writing the names of the celebrities and spaces for the teen's name and phone number. For an easier version, make a matching game with a list of the celebrities' names on the answer sheet with blanks to enter the number of the photo. The masks make this game good to use for the Halloween or Mardi Gras season and can be decorated accordingly. For Halloween, use an orange poster, Halloween border and confetti, and black masks. The poster for Mardi Gras should be colorful, using green, gold, and purple, and be decorated with feathers, sequins, and beads left over from craft projects. Feature biographies of the celebrities, books on acting, music performance, and celebrity magazines (*Teen People*, for example) in a book display. Holiday books could be added if used during Halloween or Mardi Gras. Prize ideas are posters, magazines, celebrity collector cards, or free donations from area businesses.

VARIATIONS

"Unmask the Musicians," "Unmask the Athletes," "Unmask the Politicians," and "Unmask the Authors" are all made the same way. Use any of these variations for the weeks prior to award ceremonies, play-offs, or elections.

"Who's Clowning Around?": the celebrities wear clown suits, hats cut on an Ellison or Accu-Cut machine, and circle sticker noses rather than masks.

"Name That Poet": make a collage of portraits of classical poets on a poster or bulletin board. Number each portrait. The answer sheet can either have numbered blanks to write in the names of the poets or have a list of the poets' names with blanks to write the numbers of the portraits that match.

Would photos of local celebrities or community leaders in your area make a good unmasking game?

It's a Love Match

Make a poster of pictures of famous dating or married couples individually photographed. Put numbers on the males' photos and letters on the females' photos. The object of the game is to match them up. I used celebrity couples, historical figures, and cartoon characters all on the same poster. *People Magazine* is a good source to see who is currently a couple with whom and photos can be found using a Google image search on the Internet. Answer sheets should be numbered (to represent the males) with blanks for writing the letter of the matching female and spaces for the teen's name and phone number.

Feature dating, friendship, and relationship books in a display or biographies of the people you have on the poster. This is a fun game around Valentine's Day and the prizes can be candy, music, books, stickers, or stationery with pens. A bag of small Valentine gifts can be promoted as a prize for you and your Valentine.

VARIATIONS

"Just Another Love Song": match photos of musicians with love song titles. The song titles can be glued to CD-sized circles of silver paper. Our version used red wrapping paper with a silver heart pattern for the background, CDs with red letter labels, and photos of the musicians printed in black and white with their names in red.

"Who Wrote That?": match scanned book covers with photos of the authors. The authors' names will be on the book covers already. Scan photos of the authors from book jackets or search for them on Internet author homepages. Choose books for the game that have the author's picture on the inside jacket and you will have your teens picking up those books and giving them a look!

"Who Said That?": match famous characters with famous quotes from movies and books.

"Who Sells That?": match celebrities with products they endorse.

"TV Match": match actors with their television shows and characters.

Songs Inspired by Literature

A recent Web site discovery inspired a great idea for a game and display. *The SIBL Project* (Songs Inspired By Literature) has a listing of songs, the performer, the lyrics, and the title of the book and author that inspired the song. Games could be created with scanned book covers, CDs made of silver paper with labels of the songs, photos of the authors and the singers. Any combination would make an informative, and maybe surprising, game and display.

Misheard Lyrics

Create a matching game with a list of misheard lyrics from *Kiss This Guy* and a list of the actual lyrics. Players must match them. Use when featuring a music collection or music related books. This is a fun activity at a music program where you can play the actual songs.

Play to Win

Make a poster of sports team logos. The object is to identify the team and its city by its logo. Logos may be downloaded from the Internet and any identifying words should be blacked out with a permanent marker or masked with black paper. Number the answer sheets to match the numbers on the poster with spaces to write in the city and team name. Add spaces for the teen's name and phone number. An easier version is to list the names of the teams on the answer sheet and the teens put the numbers of the posted logos that match in the blanks. Feature sports books and sports biographies. Prizes can be sports cards, sports equipment, caps, pennants, or t-shirts.

"Who Makes That?": match the company logos of favorite teen brands with the name of the company. Display business, career, fashion books, teen magazines, biographies of designers, models, inventors. Search popular magazines in the YA collection for the brands or poll the teens in your library or TAB.

What's so Great About Her?

For Women's History Month, gather photos of famous women and pictures of their accomplishments or make paper shapes with the accomplishments typed on them. Arrange on a poster or bulletin board in a mixed-up order. Number the women's photos and letter the accomplishments. The object of the game is to match the famous woman with her accomplishment. When the contest is over, match them up on the poster. An easy way to do this is to apply clear tape to the poster behind the accomplishments and using tape rolls to attach them. They can then be taped and moved and retaped to the correct positions for revealing the answers. An alternative method is making two copies of the accomplishments and posting the second copies in the correct positions over the first copies to show the answers. Feature women's biographies, women athletes, women authors, women politicians, women scientists, and women celebrities.

"Inventors Hall of Fame": make a poster with photos of famous inventors and pictures of their inventions.

TRIVIA GAMES

Trivia on many subjects provide an endless source of material for games in the YA room. You can post one question a week or several questions for the length of the program. They can be multiple-choice or fill-in-the-blank answers.

Holiday Trivia Quiz

Search for any seasonal holiday trivia questions on the Internet or in books. Cover the bulletin board with holiday wrapping paper. To make a multiple-choice trivia game, make holiday "cards" with the question printed on the front and multiple-choice answers inside and staple them to the bulletin board. Add ribbons or bows to make the bulletin board look like a wrapped gift. Wrap the drawing box to match. Answer sheets should be numbered to match the cards with blanks for the letter of the correct answers. Add spaces for the teen's name and phone number. Feature holiday books and craft books for making gifts and cards, Internet resources for finding answers. Prize ideas are stickers, candy, pins, socks, or other holiday appropriate trinkets. Several small items in a holiday gift bag makes a nice prize.

Turkey Test

Make a poster or bulletin board with a trivia test of interesting facts about turkeys for the Thanksgiving season. We had dozens of holiday turkey posters that were all the same and I put them everywhere in the YA room. The questions were found on the Internet using Google and the phrase "turkey trivia." Answer sheets should be numbered with spaces for the letter of the correct answer. Add spaces for name and phone number. Feature encyclopedias, animals and birds, Thanksgiving, autumn. A prize idea is fast food coupons (for when they've had enough turkey!).

Sports Team Trivia

"Take Me Out to the Library!": choose the favorite team in your area and look up trivia on the Internet about it. The professional and college teams all have Web sites. Post one trivia question a week for a summer program or ten trivia questions for a shorter program. Decorate with pennants, logos, sports wrapping paper. Cleveland Indians trivia was one of our first summer reading programs. Chief Wahoo dominated the YA territory that summer! A different question was posted each week. Feature the appropriate sports books, sports biographies, and team books. A fantastic prize would be tickets to a game, but make sure it is a possible opportunity for your teens to be able to go. If it would be a long trip, the expense may be too much for the winner's family to take him there. T-shirts, hats, pennants, autographs, posters, sports cards, and other sports memorabilia are all good prizes.

Library Trivia

Our first summer reading program was Library Trivia. Each week a question was posted about our own library or the employees. The answer forms went into a drawing for weekly prizes.

TV Trivia and Other Trivia Games

The Internet is a quick and easy source for many trivia quizzes on many topics. Two Web sites you may want to explore are *Surfing the Net With Kids Trivia* and *The Trivia Portal*.

GUESSING GAMES

Guessing games are fun, not requiring any real work for the teens, but can attract attention to a collection or service.

Back to School Countdown

Have a lot of something strange laying around? I had a box of almost 200 red pens, tossed them in a large gallon jar, and sealed it with book tape. The object was to guess how many pens there were. The answer sheet needs to have space for name, phone number, and a guess. The bulletin board featured all the back-to-school services we have to offer students and a book display had all the how to succeed in school and improving study skills books. The prize for this drawing was a bag of school supplies. Check the library supply closet for surplus office supplies and shop back-to-school sales. I received a shipment of school supplies from Naeir (the red pens came from that shipment) that I ended up using for several programs. What happened to the pens? I gave them to the bookmobile department to pass out to all the teachers.

VARIATIONS

Use peanuts for a circus theme, jelly beans for Easter, candy corn for a Halloween guessing game. Try office supplies, hardware, even computer chips in the jar—whatever makes a connection to the service or collection area you want to feature or fits the theme. If your YA area is not staffed, small jars of candy or nuts are not likely to survive the full length of the contest (speaks the voice of experience). Avoid tempting anyone by using items that aren't particularly useful or tasty or using a container large enough to make it too challenging to carry it out. Small jars of candy would be fine at a service desk with a drawing box for the entries. The jar of candy can be the prize.

I Spy

Take a dozen photos of buildings, sign logos, or other identifiable landmarks in your library, neighborhood, or town. Use unusual perspectives or close-ups when taking the photos. Mount the photos on a poster in a collage and number them. A digital camera and photo software can make this an interesting project with creative cropping and enlarging. The answer sheet needs to be numbered for the photos and have blanks for writing in the place where the photo was taken. Feature local history and geography, or photography and hobbies. Prize ideas are gift certificates or other giveaways donated from local businesses.

Body in the Book Drop

This was a mystery game devised by Cathy Haynes, one of our reference librarians who helped get the Teen Advisory Board started. She wrote scenarios for several of the staff member suspects explaining the circumstances of how each was responsible for the body discovered in the book drop. Photos were taken of all of the suspicious looking suspects and posted in the display case. A handout with all of the scenarios was available for each teen. A photo of the book drop with a fake arm hanging out of it and police tape all around it was in the center of the display. The teens guessed who the guilty culprit was by reading the scenarios and voting on a ballot. The actual guilty party had been determined by the staff, who eagerly voted and were entered in a drawing for a Pizza Hut gift certificate.

GIVEAWAY DRAWINGS

Giveaways are another just-for-fun program that will attract teens to the YA room. Your job is to make displays that will further attract them to the collection. Rather than just pass out the freebies to the teens, they fill out a slip for a drawing. The slips can be multi-purpose if you add a survey question or a space for an e-mail address.

Countdown to Christmas Comics Giveaway

Throughout the year I collect free comics, posters, Marvel, temporary tattoos, and collector cards from Naeir and workshops. I divide up whatever I have collected into 24 gift bags (from Naeir) and draw a winner's name every day from December 1 to 24. ALA has a poster and bookmarks with Superman and other superheroes, which is added to the display of graphic novels, comics, and how to draw and publish your own comic books. You may be able to borrow a prop from a comic store or a collector. The entry form needs space for the teen's name and phone number and his guess.

VARIATIONS

If you have access to freebies teens would like, this is a good way to distribute them. Always make the collection connection! The prize drawings will get them into the YA room, so make sure your book displays draw them to the collection.

BOOK-RELATED GAMES

The Literature Teacher's Book of Lists is a wonderful resource for book-related games. The many lists can be used for creating booklists for handouts, building collections and displays, and making games for drawing attention to them.

A few game ideas to try with some of the lists in this book or other lists you may have are:

- Shakespeare Glossary—make up the meanings of the words Balderdash®-style (see the Dictionary Game in the Lock-In and Party chapter).
- Banned Books—scan the book covers for the bulletin board display. Teens can guess which books were banned or why they were banned. Feature challenged titles and First Amendment books.
- Religious Texts—match the texts with the religion or photos of the founders. Feature books about world religions.
- Animal Symbols—match animal symbols with their meanings. Feature books on mythology and folklore.
- American Women Writers—match titles and photos of women authors.
- Which Century Was It?—a list of inventions; guess which century they were invented. Post pictures of the inventions.
- Book Terms—another Balderdash®-style game; match terms with definitions.

WORD GAMES

Word games and puzzles can be regular features in the YA room. I use them as part of the summer reading program, changing the puzzle each week. These can be adapted to any theme and any part of the library collection.

Thesaurically Speaking

Use a thesaurus to rename a list of book titles, song titles, or brand names. Post the list on the bulletin board and provide answer sheets or make a handout sheet with the synonyms and the blanks for the answers.
Examples for Christmas carols:

- Move hither the entire assembly of those who are loyal to their belief (Oh, Come All Ye Faithful).
- Vertically challenged adolescent percussionist (Little Drummer Boy).
- Allow crystalline formations to descend (Let It Snow!).
- Precious metal musical devices (Silver Bells).

Say What?

This game is all about the jargon and slang particular to any profession or group of people, including teens. Depending on the area of the collection you want to feature, choose a list of associated words and the definitions to create a matching game or let the teens guess what the words might mean.

Most sports, movie makers, computer people, business people, circuses, cowboys, even librarians (!) have special vocabularies of their own. Pocket dictionaries are fitting prizes for word games. This can also be used as a party word game.

WDIM? (What Does It Mean?)

In addition to lingo and jargon, there is the world of acronyms that separates those who know and those who don't. Try a matching game of acronyms and the definitions of what they represent. Every library system has its own set of acronyms and jargon. Give the teens an inside view of the library world by sharing those words with them. This is a fun party game, too.

Word Scrambles

If you want teens to take notice of any collection, try a word scramble game. Make a list of all the teen magazines in your collection and mix the letters up in the titles. Post on the bulletin board the numbered list of scrambled titles and provide the answer sheets numbered with blanks to write in the answers with a space for their name and phone number. It helps to have a blank for each word in the title. This game was named "The Magazine ReQuest" during our Medieval summer program. After unscrambling the titles, teens were asked to circle their favorite magazine and list a magazine they would like to see added to the collection.

Word Trivia

Many trivia games can be created from interesting words. Print up a list of words and their definitions to match or a list of words and decide what they have in common. A Collection of Word Odditites and Trivia Website has many lists of words with distinctive characteristics, such as all the vowels in the words are in alphabetical order.

Cryptograms, Crosswords, and Other Games

Puzzlemaker is an online site where you can make customized word puzzles and mazes, and print them. I have used these as part of the summer reading programs, but they can be used any time of the year for a fast handout activity or adapted to a bulletin board independent game. *Puzzlemaker* also has a nice selection of pre-made mazes and a maze generator to make your own.

Poetry Board

A poetry board is an adaptation of the magnetic poetry sets made to use on the refrigerator. I've read of a library that used a refrigerator door in the YA room for a poetry board! If you need something more portable but sturdy you can build one with plywood. Cut the plywood to whatever shape and size will work in the YA room. Staple low napped carpet to the front and bind the edges with heavy book binding tape. A lighter, less durable version can be made with a few sheets of cardboard layered together, taped, and covered with carpet. The words are composed on a word processor in a large font and printed on card stock. Colored paper for seasonal words looks nice and cheery. Cut the words apart and place them close together face down on a piece of contact paper and cover with another piece of the contact paper. Cut the words apart and attach a piece of the hook side of Velcro to the back. The words are durable and can be moved around freely over the board. As a collection of words are accumulated, they may be kept in a basket or box by the poetry board. Some libraries have carpeted walls so a lot of the work is done already! Your poetry board can be moved to a poetry program, or moved in and out of the YA room at different times of the year.

VIRTUAL MAKEOVER DAY

Load the Cosmopolitan Virtual Makeover 3.5 CD in a PC with a color printer. Take a picture of each teen with a digital camera, load it into the program and teens can try on hundreds of new looks. The CD is available from Amazon.com and costs about $20.00 or may be borrowed from a library collection. Teens can schedule appointments after school or on a Saturday for their Virtual Makeover Day.

CONTESTS

Contests give teens an opportunity to test their artistic and writing skills, enjoy a bit of competition, and see their work displayed in the public forum. Enlist the aid of your library director, school art teachers, art museum curator, local art, photography, or writing club members to help with judging and decide on the type of contest by the expertise you have available to you. You may like to display all the entries and have the patrons vote for their favorite for a "Reader's Choice" award.

Decide on a theme, size requirements, media, number of entries from each contestant, age range of the contestants, and any other restrictions to narrow the range of entries you will receive. Set a deadline, judging period, and date for announcing the winner. Consider your own deadline for publication or printing of the winning entry when scheduling the contest. Then allow four weeks between first announcing the contest and the deadline for entries. Make up flyers with an official entry form that includes all the information you would need for announcing and informing the winners. The actual prize may be using the art work for publicizing a special program, making book marks for the library from the original work, or publication in the library newsletter. A cash or gift certificate award is nice to offer if you have the funds or can get someone to sponsor the contest like a local art supply store, stationery store, or bookstore.

Photography

Photo entries of patrons using the library can be used for the National Library Week display and bookmarks. A local business may offer free film or developing as a prize.

Posters

In the spring, use the Summer Reading Program theme to design a poster for Summer Reading Promotion. National Library Week or Teen Read Week are other occasions for a poster contest. Another theme for posters is making a movie poster promoting your favorite book. The contest should run for several weeks before the event so the winners can be announced and the artwork can be used to publicize the event.

Poetry

Publish the winning poem in the library's newsletter for National Poetry Month or publish all entries in an annual booklet for distribution in the young adult room. Try Haiku or Tanka around Chinese New Year and limerick contests for Saint Patrick's Day or a patriotic poem for Independence Day.

Essay

Submit the winning essay to a local newspaper for Teen Read Week. Try "Growing Up in the Library," "What the Library Means To Me," "How the Library Changed My Life," or a topic chosen by the TAB.

Bookmarks

Design a bookmark to be used throughout a season or program. The original can be taken to a professional printer, or scanned and reprinted on a laser printer, depending on your budget.

THE BOTTOM LINE

Independent programs are almost free to put together, using materials you can find in your library or on the Internet, and the contests use items produced by the teens. Prizes will be your expense and you may be able to get donations from local businesses in exchange for recognition in your publicity. Inexpensive small prizes are fine for independent programs. Take a teen shopping with you or ask your teen board for suggestions if you have no idea what they would like. Pass catalogs around at TAB meetings and give the teens a prize budget and let them choose the prizes. Offer coupons for library fines, replacement cards, or any services that would normally cost money. Some libraries prefer the draw of one big prize. If you have the connections to get a large prize donated to the library, then it makes sense to use it. TVs, bikes, scooters, or boom boxes would please most any teen. Keep in mind only teens that really want that particular prize are likely to enter since the competition is greater for one prize. Big prizes are great for advertising a program, but in the end only one teen is going to be rewarded and happy.

THE COLLECTION CONNECTION

These sample independent programs have suggestions of collections you can feature with them. Explore other areas of your collection to develop other matching or trivia games and contests.

RESOURCES

The Alternative Dictionaries [Online]. Available: www.notam02.no/~hcholm/altlang/ [2002, May 10].

Arthur Elementary School. 2001. *Trivia Quizzes and Hunts* [Online]. Available: www.arthur.k12.il.us/arthurgs/trivia.htm [2002, May 10].

A Collection of Word Oddities and Trivia [Online]. Available: http://members.aol.com/ gulfhigh2/words.html [2002, May 10].

Dictionary of British Slang [Online]. Available: www.peevish.co.uk/slang/ [2002, May 10].

Discovery School's Puzzle Maker [Online]. Available: www.puzzlemaker.com/ [2002, May 10].

Distinguished Women of Past and Present [Online]. Available: www.DistinguishedWomen.com [2002, May 10].

Google [Online]. Available: www.google.com [2002, May 10]. I always use the advanced search to narrow down my results. The image search is great for finding pictures for posters and bulletin boards.

High Quality Football Logos [Online]. Available: www.hqfl.dk/ [2002, May 10].

Kiss This Guy [Online]. Available: www.kissthisguy.com/ [2002, May 10].

National Inventors Hall of Fame [Online]. Available: www.invent.org/hall_of_fame/ 1_0_0_hall_of_fame.asp [2002, May 10].

The SIBL Project: Songs Inspired By Literature [Online]. Available: www.siblproject.org/ [2002, May 10].

The Sports Logo Arena [Online]. Available: www.geocities.com/Colosseum/Arena/ 2936/index.html [2002, May 10].

Strouf, Judie L. H. 1997. *The Literature Teacher's Book of Lists*. New York: The Center for Applied Research in Education.

Surfing the Net With Kids Trivia Games [Online]. Available: www.surfnetkids.com/games/Trivia_Games/ [2002, May 10].

The Trivia Portal [Online]. Available: www.funtrivia.com/ [2002, May 10].

Whiteley, Sandy. 2002. *Chase's Calendar of Events 2002*. New York: McGraw-Hill.

Chapter 5

Craft Programs

OVERVIEW

Craft programs are fun social activities and learning experiences for the teens and their librarians. They inspire creativity, can be inexpensive, and the teens go home with a nice homemade gift for themselves or someone else. Crafts can be part of a larger program like a lock-in, a short after-school, make-it and take-it program, or a longer Saturday program for bigger messier projects. Depending on the complexity of the project, the make it and take it program can be one to two hours long. Pre-registration is helpful for craft programs to determine the amount of materials you will need to collect. Don't forget the snacks—creativity makes teens hungry!

Collect craft ideas from magazines, the Internet, friends, co-workers, listservs, local crafts people, and use your own favorite crafts. Crafts that produce a nice project even if the teen isn't particularly artistic are best, and it makes the project easier for you, too, if you don't feel you are creative! Crafts provide an opportunity to teach in a variety of styles: teens will learn from you, from each other, and on their own.

A COLLECTION OF CRAFT PROGRAMS

The following craft projects are a lot of fun for the relatively small investment of materials. The choices the teens make in colors and designs will ensure each teen will go home with an original work, different from everyone else's.

Beads! Beads! Beads!

Beads! Beads! Beads! was our first make it and take it craft program for teens. It works well for an after-school program. Twenty-five girls and guys came for our two-hour event and most of them stayed and worked on projects the entire two hours. It was held on a Thursday from 4–6 p.m. in mid November. The publicity suggested teens could come to make a gift for the holidays.

Figure 5–1 Bead Program Publicity Display.
A display with samples of the craft projects will attract teen attention. Many adults wanted to sign up after seeing the projects the teens would be making!

Ask friends, family, and co-workers for leftover bead project materials and spend your budget on what you need to make them into projects teens might like. The tools we needed were collected from the library workroom and at home and many beads were donated by co-workers and my daughter's family, and I had a few at home. The rest of the beads, the hemp, and the suede cord were purchased from Wal-Mart. I had a box of prism Christmas ornaments from Naeir. My daughter had described the pretty (and expensive) beaded prisms she had seen at a Renaissance Festival, so I added the prisms to the supplies. Similar acrylic prism ornaments may be found after the holiday season on sale in discount and department stores.

The diameter of the hole on the beads needs to match the size of the material you are using for stringing them. Tiny beads fit on fine wire or fishing line. The medium beads work on hemp and heavier wire and the larger beads fit on the suede cord.

Display the materials and copies of patterns on a table with samples of each project you make ahead of time. I had provided the materials and patterns for key rings, bracelets, tribal belts, chokers, prism ornaments, and star ornaments. The resource list will show you where to find these and other

Figure 5–2 Bead Program.
Serve up a selection of beads and patterns! The teens choose their own project and their own beads for truly unique designs.

patterns. The teens choose the beads with a divided Styrofoam plate in hand, cafeteria style, and then go to a table to work. Display bead craft books and serve simple refreshments. We had cider, root beer, donuts, and pretzels. I was the only staff member present and I floated around helping with macramé knots and explaining project details when needed.

MATERIALS NEEDED

Many beads displayed in baby food jars or coffee cups, plastic spoons for scooping out small beads, projects made up for examples, copies of instructions, wire (heavier and fine jewelry wire), fishing line, scissors, wire cutters, needle nosed or jewelers pliers (available at craft stores), masking tape (for taping ends of macramé projects to the table), rulers, yard stick, foam divided plates or muffin tins, key rings, necklace latches, suede cord, prisms, and hemp.

THE BOTTOM LINE

This project can vary a great deal in cost, depending upon the selection of beads and variety of project patterns you want to offer. I spent less than $50.00 on the whole program and each teen took home several projects. Some supplies are left for another beading program. To cut expenses, offer fewer types of projects and buy the less expensive packages of beads. I found beads that looked like footballs and basketballs that are made for shoe ties (that were popular for making key rings for boyfriends) at the Flower Factory, a craft store. Initial beads were also popular for bracelets and key rings and any unusual beads were used up first.

THE COLLECTION CONNECTION

Display books on beads, macramé, and crafts, Internet craft sites, and magazines with crafts. A bead activity could be added to a multi-cultural program as a Native American craft.

Mehndi Tattoo and a Taste of India

Mehndi is the ancient art of making temporary tattoos by staining the skin with henna paste. Mehndi is fun and easy to learn how to do. I learned out of necessity when my presenter cancelled two weeks before the program! My daughter, Lori, came to the rescue and agreed to learn how to do it with me. I reserved all the books in the online catalog, read several sites on the Internet, and ordered the easiest kits I could find. The Mehndi Tattoo and a Taste of India program was held on a Saturday through lunch time from 11 a.m. to 2 p.m. so an Indian meal could be served (which I learned to prepare in those same two weeks!).

I found mehndi kits at www.thehennapeople.com that included pre-made paste in a tube with an application tip and stencils, which are nice for the non-artistic teens that want a pretty elaborate tattoo. One kit per two tattoo artists is enough, as it is easier to work on someone else than it is on yourself and the stencils are reusable. Lori experimented on all her friends and in the meantime, I experimented on my co-workers, who were good sports to be walking ads for the program. Lori purchased the dried henna and oil to mix to compare with the pre-made paste after experimenting with the tubes. This mixture stained darker and lasted a little longer, but took a little more artistic talent to apply. She brought the dried henna and a prepared mixture to the program so the teens got to see and smell the henna. They enjoyed painting on the mixed henna with paintbrushes, cotton swabs, and toothpicks.

Introduce the program by explaining a little history about mehndi and sharing a few of the traditions from the books and sites you visit. Show your tattoos so the teens can see what their finished tattoos will look like. Distribute the materials to each table with books of designs from the collection or borrowed from other libraries. Provide step-by-step instructions for the procedure so teens can work independently.

Mehndi

Mehndi is the ancient art of henna tattooing. Traditionally, a bride's hands are tattooed before the wedding and she does no housework until the tattoos fade, usually two-three weeks! The bride can hide the name of her groom in the tattoo and if he cannot find it, she will rule the household!

How To Do Mehndi

1. Choose a design or stencil.
2. Wash the area to be tattooed with a cotton ball and lemon juice. This removes skin oils and lotions. Dry skin.
3. Apply stencil if using one. Then apply the henna. Drink a warm drink.
4. Let dry. You may use a hair dryer for this step.
5. Apply lemon sugar glaze every half hour or so.
6. Leave henna on at least two hours. Remove stencil once henna is good and dry.
7. Scrape off dried henna. Use water sparingly. Apply food oil or essential oil, not baby oil.

Figure 5–3 Mehndi Instructions Handout.
A handout of step-by-step instructions helps teens work on their own and have good results tattooing each other.

Figure 5–4 Mehndi Program.
The teens enjoy trying traditional designs and creating their own.

A few of the teens were discovered to be talented with their original designs and became very busy tattooing others! Lori, her friend Matt, and I were all busy tattooing as well, but everyone gave it a try. Lori also brought bindi, the stick on designs that are traditionally for the center of the forehead, but Madonna and other stars have incorporated bindi into their more elaborate tattoo designs. The teens loved this program and went home with tattoos and several bindi all over them. They would have stayed longer if parents hadn't been waiting.

MATERIALS NEEDED

Mehndi kits, lemon juice, toothpicks, cotton swabs, paper towels, hair dryer (to speed up the drying process), lemon/sugar glaze (heat lemon juice in microwave and dissolve equal amount of sugar in it), and copies of the instructions for each teen.

THE TASTE OF INDIA MEAL

My presenter was going to provide food too, so I had to decide what to do about a lunch. I chose a simple to prepare Indian recipe that I found in children's and young adult international cookbooks. To prepare the meal, buy packages of saffron rice that only need to be boiled with water, Archway coconut macaroons, and ready-made pita pockets. Cut up a cantaloupe and a honeydew melon and make chicken curry and keep it hot in a crock pot. An important part of a curry meal is the condiments, so provide eight small bowls of condiments: coconut, raisins, chopped peanuts, chutney, chopped tomatoes, chopped green pepper, chopped hard cooked egg, and chopped onion. If you have an international grocery store or an Indian grocery in your area, you can be more adventurous with your meal! The teens were free to fill up a plate any time during the program. I used brightly patterned shiny wrapping paper for table covers and books about India and Indian cooking for decorations. India travel videos playing in the background provided music and some cultural education. The teens filled their senses with the taste and smells and looks of India.

Figure 5–5 Chicken Curry Meal.
An Indian chicken curry meal will add cultural atmosphere to a mehndi program.

THE BOTTOM LINE

The mehndi kits were discounted when buying a dozen. I purchased 12 kits for $108.00, which was enough for the program and practicing. The prepared henna in tubes has preservatives that make it not stain as effectively as the dried henna. The dried henna that you mix with oil is less expensive, but takes a more practiced hand to get good results. The older teens had good luck with it, while the younger teens liked the tubes with the applicator tips better. Bindi and the Indian meal are extras to add if you have the money.

It isn't necessary to serve a whole meal with the tattooing program, but do provide snacks and a warm drink. The warm drink raises the body temperature, which helps the henna to stain better. I had donated the ingredients for this meal and took home the leftovers for a yummy feast the next day.

THE COLLECTION CONNECTION

Display books on India, mehndi, Celtic designs, Chinese calligraphy, Indian cooking, tattooing, Hindi writing, Egyptian hieroglyphics, travel videos, and Internet sites about mehndi.

Sand Art and Sand Painting

Our sand art project was part of the Beach Party Lock-In program, but could easily be a make-it and take-it craft for after school or part of a multi-cultural program. I used containers and tools on hand and purchased the colored sand. The style we used was pouring colors in a jar layer by layer and making designs with the tools.

We used junior-sized baby food jars donated by a staff member for our containers. I spray painted the lids and hot glued small shells, stones, and fossils (that I had at home) on them ahead of time. If you have enough time during the program, the gluing can be done then. However, if your jars are all the same size, the teens can spend their time on the sand art and just choose a finished lid they like to top it off.

The tools can be any shape that has a handle long enough to reach down the sides of the jar. Spoons and forks and wooden skewers are all helpful tools. The different colors of sand were poured into separate bowls and spoons were placed in them for adding small amounts of sand to the jars one at a time. I had a bag of aquarium gravel at home so I poured it into a sand bucket. A gravel layer added an interesting texture change in among the sand layers. It is important to make sure the jars are filled all the way to the top so the sand has no room to shift after the lid is put on. The lids may be hot glued on to keep them sealed. Every sand art jar will have its own unique look when finished. Pictures of landscapes, geological strata, or geometric designs may be used to inspire creativity. Fake jewels, buttons, or beads are good decorations to glue on top, too. Purchased jars with corks from craft stores can also be used for the containers.

The same colored sand can be used to make sand paintings, called mandalas. The mandalas created by Tibetan monks take nine days to create and are destroyed when finished, but our version is quicker and a little more permanent. Recently, the Dalai Lama called for healing mandalas to be made in the aftermath of the September 11th attack.

You will need the colored sand in separate bowls with spoons and Popsicle sticks, Elmer's glue, and small paintbrushes. Pencils, compasses, rulers, and geometric templates are all helpful drawing aids for the design. Traditional mandala designs are symmetrical and a simple design is easier to do than an intricate one. Provide scratch paper for developing a design and heavier paper or cardstock for the final design. Photos of authentic mandalas from books and the Internet can provide inspiration.

When the design is drawn on the cardstock, glue is painted in a very thin layer in one area of the design at a time. The desired color of sand is spooned on and the extra is poured off back into the bowl. Pour the sand on again to make sure every bit of the glue is covered. Proceed to another section of the design using the same color. A cleaner finished design will result if the teen waits for the glue to dry when finished applying one color before proceeding to a different color. When the painting is finished, it may be sealed with artist's fixative.

Sand painting done by the Navajos includes other natural materials, such as cornmeal and seeds, and are created and destroyed within 12 hours. African cultures also make sand paintings, each one telling a story. Do a bit of research on the Internet about the type of sand painting you want to present so you can make your program educational as well as fun. A few links are included in the list of resources at the end of the chapter.

MATERIALS NEEDED

Colored sand in bowls with spoons, small clear containers with lids, design tools, spray paint and decorations for lids or cork stoppers, hot glue gun for the poured jar lids, pencils, compasses, rulers and geometric templates, and paper and card stock for the paintings.

THE BOTTOM LINE

Colored sand is inexpensive for a small group and is available at many craft stores. Most of the other materials are available at your library or through donations from staff, family, and friends. An alternative to using colored sand is using colored salt for the jars. A quick and easy method to color salt is to pour the salt into a bowl and stir it with an artist's grade chalk until the salt is the desired color. Sidewalk chalk will work also, but the colors will be pastel. The colored salt is not suitable for the paintings.

THE COLLECTION CONNECTION

Sand painting is a multi-cultural art form and the paintings have spiritual meanings in their native cultures. Depending on the style of sand art you present, you could use this activity in a program about Native American, African, or Far Eastern art, spiritualism, or culture. Share a bit of history and pictures of traditional designs at the beginning of the program. Collect books and photos from the Internet to illustrate the style of sand painting you want to present. Books with traditional cultural art designs will inspire the teens to create their own meaningful artwork. Sand art is also just fun and can be part of a lock-in program or adapted to any summer reading program theme. I used it at the Beach Party to incorporate the idea of a sandy beach.

Tie Dye

Tie dying is a fun, productive, and messy activity . . . perfect for teens. Our tie dye event took place on the Saturday before Valentine's Day from 11 a.m. to 1 p.m. Teens can tie dye at least two t-shirts in an hour, so this would be a good after-school or lock-in program, too.

I ordered a kit from Dharma Trading Company. Their catalog lists several group kits; the one I chose included ingredients to tie dye up to 50 t-shirts. The kit contained three jars of powdered dye, a bag of soda ash, a bag of urea, several pairs of latex gloves, a bag of rubber bands, six 16-oz. plastic applicator bottles, and a book of design instructions. The teens were instructed to bring an item to tie dye when they signed up for the program. Shirts, socks, and pillowcases are all easy to manage.

The work area was set up with four large tables pushed together and covered with plastic tablecloths. Use the wrong side of the tablecloths if there is a color design on them so the pattern will not bleed onto the shirts.

MATERIALS NEEDED

Place the following items on the tables:

- Latex gloves
- Rolls of paper towels
- Piles of rubber bands
- Bowls of water for rinsing fingers between colors
- Bottles of mixed dye
- Copies of tying instructions
- Plastic grocery bags

Place on a plastic tablecloth on the floor nearby:

- 2 buckets of soda ash solution
- 1 bucket clear water for rinsing hands
- An old towel for drying hands and wiping up drips

The following step-by-step instructions were written on flip chart paper and taped to the walls on both sides of the room so they wouldn't get lost among all the other materials.

Dying Instructions
1. Choose a design. Fold your t-shirt and bind it with rubber bands according to the instructions for that design. 2. Soak the shirt in the soda ash solution for 5-10 minutes, until it is saturated. 3. Squeeze out excess solution. 4. Take shirt to the table, put on gloves, and apply dye. 5. Place shirt in plastic bag.

Figure 5–6 Tie Dye Instructions.
Post the dying instructions on the wall so they won't get lost on the table!

Washing instructions were printed on half sheets of paper and available on the refreshment table. Teens were reminded before leaving to pick one up so they would know how to finish the project the next day at home.

Washing Instructions
1. Leave shirt in bag for 12 to 24 hours. 2. Rinse off excess dye under warm running water. 3. Cut off rubber bands and continue rinsing until the water runs clear. 4. Wash shirt separately in hot water and dry as usual. Don't let the shirt set before washing or dye will run and stain other areas of your shirt. 5. After washing and drying, the shirt is safe to put in the regular laundry.

Figure 5–7 Tie Dye Washing Instructions.
Make sure the teens take home a sheet of washing instructions to finish their tie dye project.

Simple refreshments were served on a separate table: pretzels, Oreos, Valentine candy, and red punch.

THE BOTTOM LINE

A kit to dye up to 50 t-shirts costs $50.00 from Dharma Trading. This provided enough ingredients for two small group programs. Providing t-shirts would add a great expense unless you can get a donation. Asking the teens to bring something to tie dye gives them even more room to be creative.

Soaps and Lotions/Aromatherapy

Making soaps, lotion, and bath salts is not only easy and economical, but educational and fun. The teens can customize their own line of bath products for a gift or for themselves. The popularity of bathing products stores in malls guarantees an interest in this program. A gift basket can be made with a plastic strawberry basket lined with excelsior, Easter grass, or cellophane paper. A ribbon that coordinates with the bath products can be woven through the basket and tied in a bow.

MATERIALS NEEDED

You need inexpensive unscented white lotion, food coloring, cosmetic grade fragrance or essential oils, and glycerin soap blocks. Collect small plastic containers (yogurt, ice cream, or small margarine containers) with smooth insides for soap molds and baby food jars with painted lids for lotion. Move a microwave oven into the room to melt the soap. A Pyrex measuring cup is perfect to melt the soap in the oven. Use plastic spoons for stirring; do not use metal or wood utensils or containers. Use unflavored cooking spray to coat the soap molds. Collect plain white address labels, permanent colored pens, plastic wrap, small disposable bowls, or cereal bowls. If making bath salts, add a carton of Epsom salts and sandwich bags.

PROCEDURES

Procedure for soaps: The soap comes in two-pound blocks that can be sliced with a knife into equal-sized blocks for each teen. Melt a block in the microwave in the Pyrex measuring cup. This should take less than 30 seconds, and the soap should be the consistency of gravy. Add a few drops of food coloring, one at a time, for desired color. Add up to five drops of scent and stir. If you let the soap get too hot, let it cool a little before adding scent so it won't evaporate too quickly. Spray the soap mold lightly with cooking spray. Pour the soap into the mold and let set. Design a label with permanent pens, unmold, and wrap cooled solid soap with saran wrap and seal with the label.

Procedure for lotions: Pour the amount of lotion into a bowl that will fill the baby food jar. (Fill the jar with water and pour it into a measuring cup to see how much lotion you need.) Add one or two drops of food coloring for desired color, add up to five drops of scent. Stir and pour into the baby food jar. Design a label with permanent pens and stick label on the side of the jar. Jewels or beads can be hot glued to the lids.

Procedure for bath salts: Fill a baby food jar with Epsom salts, then pour the salt into a sandwich bag. Add 2–3 drops of color and scent, secure the top of the bag, and shake until the color is even. Pour the salt into a baby food jar and label and decorate the lid to coordinate with the lotion.

For extra pizzazz: Iridescent cosmetic powders and glitters may be added to the soaps and lotions, and oatmeal can be added to the soap. The oatmeal can be ground finer in a blender or with a mortar and pestle. A contrasting color of soap confetti can be added right before pouring the soap into the mold. To make the confetti, melt a small chunk of soap and add food coloring; the color should be a little more intense for the confetti. Pour onto a plate or countertop in a thin layer. When cooled, cut into small pieces or shapes and add to the melted soap. Tiny spirals can be made by cutting slivers and shaping them with your fingers. The pieces will melt if added when the base soap is too hot! Freezing the small pieces a few minutes will help them keep their shape when added to the melted soap.

Make the soap first so it can set up while the teens make the lotion, salts, and labels. An emphasis on aromatherapy can be made by using the essential oils for fragrance and telling the teens what each fragrance is supposed to do.

THE BOTTOM LINE

You can save money or spend more on this project by choosing purchased manufactured molds or saving containers you can collect for free. Plastic yogurt containers, small ice cream cups, or small margarine tubs work well. Food coloring from home is as effective and safe as the cosmetic grade colors. Soap can be purchased on the Internet for about $2.50 a pound, which will make four bars or more if using smaller molds. Buying in larger quantities is cheaper per pound. Inexpensive body lotion or hand creams work well—just choose a product with the consistency you want the finished lotion to have from your local discount store. If you want to spend more, you can also purchase little bottles for the lotion. Epsom salts can be found in drug or grocery stores. I purchased sea salt kits at the Flower Factory that included enough scent and color to use in the soaps and lotions, too.

THE COLLECTION CONNECTION

Books on making soaps, lotions, and homemade cosmetics, beauty, grooming, skin care, makeup, makeovers, aromatherapy, and fashion magazines.

MORE CRAFT PROGRAM IDEAS

Candle Making

I made several kinds of candles as a teen using the paraffin used to seal jelly jars and melted broken crayons in it for color. Close supervision is needed for the melting process as the paraffin is flammable. A double boiler method is safer than direct heat. A coffee can in a large pot with water in it over a low to medium heat works well as a melter.

Sand candles are made by scooping out a bowl shape in a bucket of damp sand and pushing fingers down into the sand to create three-leg molds for the candle. A wick tied to a stick bridges the scooped out area and the melted colored paraffin is poured into the hollowed area. When the candle cools and is lifted out of the bucket, it has a coating of sand on the outside and has three legs to stand on.

An interesting candle can be made by filling a half-gallon milk or juice carton with ice cubes around a colored taper candle in the center. Plain white paraffin is poured over the ice to the top of the taper. When cooled, the carton is torn away and the water poured off. The ice leaves odd shaped holes in the white outside layer so the colored taper can be seen.

A special effect can be achieved by whipping up melted paraffin and scooping it with an ice cream dipper. An ice cream cone can be dipped in paraffin and filled with melted paraffin and a scoop of the whipped paraffin added on top.

There are many books and Internet sites on the many varieties of homemade candles and instructions on how to make them. Check the Web sites in the Resources list at the end of the chapter for a start. Gel candles, soy candles, and beeswax sheets that you just roll up are all possibilities for a candle-making program. Waxes that melt at lower temperatures than paraffin are available. They are better for filling containers because they will not keep their shapes.

Candy Making

Molded chocolates are very simple to make. Borrow molds from friends, co-workers, and family or purchase at a crafts store. Melting chocolate comes in wafers that melt quickly and are easy to pour and handle. The basic process is melt and pour the chocolate into molds, freeze a few minutes, and pop out of the molds. Many variations can be added to make the program more fun (and messier). The chocolate is melted in a double boiler or microwave. Pastel-colored and white chocolate can be melted and used to paint the inside of the molds with small paintbrushes before pouring in the chocolate to make fancier candies for holidays or special occasions. Peanut butter cups, coconut haystacks, and pecan turtles all have easy to make fillings and are quick to assemble.

- Peanut butter cups: Mix together 1/3 c. peanut butter and 2-1/2 T. powdered sugar. Form into small balls and slightly flatten. Pour a small amount of melted chocolate in a paper candy cup, let harden for a minute, then place the peanut butter fondant on top. Fill with more melted chocolate. Chill until hardened.
- Coconut haystacks: Mix toasted coconut with melted chocolate and spoon into mounds and chill.
- Pecan turtles: The day before making the turtles, make the caramel by boiling an unopened can of Eagle Brand sweetened condensed milk for three hours. Refrigerate overnight. You will have made the caramel filling. Arrange five whole pecans to form the legs and head of a turtle. The pecans should be almost touching each other. Spoon a small puddle of melted chocolate in the middle and chill a few minutes. Place a small spoon of caramel in the middle of the chocolate and pour more melted chocolate over the caramel. The turtle's feet and head should still peek out from the chocolate shell.

Candy making can be part of a chocolate party, a lock-in activity, or an after-school craft. Christmas, Valentine's Day, and Easter are all holiday times connected with chocolate candy. Teens could also make the candy for a children's program or to sell as a fund-raiser.

Scrapbook Picture Frames

The scrap booking projects described in craft books take a bit of time, but all the papers, stickers, fancy scissors, and other trimmings always look so fun. I have accumulated several 5" x 7" picture frames, the folding cardboard kind that most people throw away when they buy a real frame. You may discover your co-workers and relatives have lots of these laying around, or you might construct your own from lightweight cardboard.

The photo sizes will determine the size you want to cut the cardboard. For a 5" x 7" photo, cut one piece of cardboard 14" x 9". Fold in half to measure 7" x 9." Cut another piece 7" x 9". The second piece is the part that will frame the photo. Use a ruler or curved guide to draw an opening for the photo and cut carefully along the line with an Exacto knife. On the wrong side of the cardboard, draw a line of white glue around three sides of the frame 1/4" from the edge and glue to the right inside of the larger piece of cardboard. When dry, the photo can slip into the open side.

These make fun picture frames decorated with all the trimmings of a scrap book page, with the paper and stickers matching the theme of the photograph. Patterns to cut the fancy paper to fit the inside and outside of the frames are needed (just use one of the frames you made) and a good supply of interesting papers and stickers, borrowed fancy scissors from scrap book hobbyists, and gel pens for lettering. Rubber cement or glue sticks are neater than white glue for the papers. Frames are fun to create for photos of pets, sports, band, and prom.

Make a Journal

Journals can be made with materials available at home and in the library. A journal or book making project can be part of a writing workshop series or combined with a paper making project. The following instructions for completing one 32-page journal are adapted from instructions provided by Bonnie Herrage of Cuyahoga County Public Library. Bonnie has used the journal project in her series of workshops geared to girls.

The materials needed are cardboard at least 3/16" thick, wallpaper or fabric for a cover, 1/4" wide ribbon, three pieces of 8 1/2" x 11" parchment or other durable paper for the end sheets, 16 sheets of 8 1/2" x 11" paper for the writing pages, and glue, scissors, embroidery floss, and a needle for assembly.

1. Cut two pieces of cardboard 5-1/2" wide by 9" high for the front and back covers, and one piece 1/2" wide and 9" high for the spine.
2. Cut fabric or wallpaper 15" wide by 12" high. Press the fabric if needed.
3. Spread out the fabric and arrange the cover pieces with the spine in the middle. Align the cardboard pieces evenly on the fabric and apply glue about 1" inside the edges of the cardboard.
4. Fold the top of the fabric over the glue on the cardboard. Fold the fabric over the bottom edge. Fold in the sides, miter folding the corners. Be sure the edges and corners are secure, adding more glue if necessary
5. Glue a 15" piece of ribbon halfway down the inside of the spine so the end will extend past the top of the book.
6. Glue one sheet of parchment paper over the exposed cardboard. The cover of the book is completed.
7. Fold the remaining two sheets of parchment paper in half. Glue half of one sheet to the inside front of the book and one half of the other sheet to the inside back of the book, the folds along the spine. These are the end sheets.
8. Fold the 16 sheets of 8-1/2" x 11" paper in half to 8-1/2" x 5-1/2," and divide into four groups of four sheets of paper tucked inside each other.

9. Thread two strands of floss through a needle and do not tie a knot. Leaving an end for tying off, push the needle through the fold near the bottom edge. Then push the needle through the fold near the top edge. Tie a knot to secure the pages together. Repeat for the other three groups of paper.
10. Glue each section along the fold to the spine of the book between the end pages. Hold until the glue sets.
11. Fabric paint, sequins, and lace trims can be used to decorate the front cover, if desired.

Mardi Gras Masks

Offer feathers, beads, sequins, fake jewels, plastic coins, glitter, ribbon, foil paper and mylar scraps, tinsel, bead garlands, lamé and velvet scraps, buttons, tacky glue (works best with these materials), and plain white or black eye masks to decorate. The colors of Mardi Gras are purple, gold, and green. These masks are beautiful to wear or hang on the wall. A box of odds and ends craft supplies can be used for this project or new supplies can be purchased at craft stores. The masks can be purchased online at Oriental Trading Company for about $1.25 per dozen and up. Cat eye masks in Mardi Gras colors are also available.

TEEN FEEDBACK

• I liked doing the henna tattoos! That was fun! You got to pick any design you wanted and put it on your body somewhere! I liked it a lot! I hope we have it again because I will come!—Shaleen Young

RESOURCES

Candle Teacher [Online]. Available: www.candleteacher.com/ [2002, May 11].
Candyland Crafts [Online]. Available: www.candylandcrafts.com/candy_making.html [2002, May 11].
Dharma Trading [Online]. Available: www.dharmatrading.com/ [2002, May 11].
Early Tibetan Mandalas: The Rossi Collection [Online]. Available: www.asianart.com/mandalas/mandimge.html [2002, May 11].
The Henna People [Online]. Available: www.thehennapeople.com [2002, May 11].
Kiva's American India Symbol Disctionary [Online]. Available: www.kivatrading.com/symbol1.htm [2002, July 31].
Making Friends [Online]. Available: www.MakingFriends.com [2002, May 11].
The Melting Pot [Online]. Available: www.angelfire.com/ca/SSaSSSy/candle.html [2002, May 11].
Snowdrift Farms Natural Products [Online]. Available: www.snowdriftfarm.com [2002, May 11].

Soap Wizards [Online]. Available: www.soapwizards.com [2002, May 11].

"Star Bright." 2001. *American Girl* 9, no. 6 (November/December): 34–35.

Symbolism of the Mandalas [Online]. Available: www.buddhanet.net/mandalas.htm [2002, May 11].

Van Den Beukel, Dorine. 2000. *Traditional Mehndi Designs: A Treasury of Henna Body Art.* Boston: Shambhala.

Chapter 6

Game Programs

OVERVIEW

Games are a fun addition to a get together or can be the central part of a program. Put new twists to familiar board games or TV game shows to catch the teens' interest because they know how the familiar version of the game is played. Your Teen Advisory Board can help brainstorm ideas for games and how to play them, as well. The games can be made to fit many themes including books, library knowledge, and pop culture; all is needed is your imagination and the Internet or books for sources for questions.

A COLLECTION OF GAME PROGRAMS

These games are fun, challenging, creative, educational, and social. Games use skills in logic or require a bit of learning and knowledge, and all should include some humor!

ROLE-PLAYING GAMES

Role-playing games continue to be popular with teens. They are storytelling games where every player writes the story. The players develop their own characters and have a fantasy adventure following a complex set of rules. Generally, the games are played in rounds. The order of play is decided with rolls of the many sided dice. There are series of books available for role-playing games, including Dungeons and Dragons, Warhammer, RIFTS, Shadowrun, and Magic: The Gathering. Ask your teens or comic shop owner which ones are popular in your area. A book store or comic shop owner that sells role-playing books and supplies will know local gamers and can connect you with someone that can help you start a group or may offer to come and teach teens to play.

Our library hosted two Dungeons and Dragons nights during our Medieval Summer Reading Program. My son-in-law was enlisted to be the Dungeon Master and wrote an adventure that could be completed in two nights. The teens were pleased to meet new players and spent four hours both nights absorbed in the campaign. My only contribution was supplying snacks and I brought in all the D&D books in our collection.

The popularity of this program led to the formation of a Role Playing Club that meets weekly at the library. One of the TAB members organizes the group. They play an ongoing adventure game and all I do is book the meeting room and provide a bag of snacks and a bottle of soda and they spend three-four hours playing. They order their own pizzas and I save coupons for them. The group grew enough to split in two and now we have two role-playing clubs meeting weekly. When new fantasy and role-playing books come in, I show them to these groups first. Several of the role players have become interested in other activities and programs at the library. They have had a chance to get to know me and hear about the other programs by being at

Figure 6–1 Warhammer Role Players.
These Warhammer fans say they like the strategy and the playing pieces in this role-playing game.

the library more often. A few are also members of the TAB and have enjoyed giving me tips on what to add to our fantasy collection.

Figure 6–2 Dungeons and Dragons Role Players.
Dungeons and Dragons and other fantasy role-playing games appeal to creative teens who say they find them more satisfying than video games.

Purchased Mystery Games

Purchased role-playing games can be used for lock-ins or mystery nights. How To Host a Mystery and Double Dog Press Mystery Night kits provide scripts, characters, and methods for playing. This type of role-playing game is meant to be played in one evening. Put together a Mystery Dinner Night with one of these kits by adding pizza or subs and sodas.

Live Clue

Live Clue is my own creation based on the Clue® board game. The teens are the suspects and six rooms of the library become the game board. If you have never played the Clue® board game, it is recommended that you do before putting a live version together so it will make sense. While this game takes a bit of preparation, it is free if you use what you have on hand or can borrow for setting up the crime scenes. The clue collecting notebooks are made from paper and cardboard and the weapons are made from cardboard and aluminum foil and dowels. The game will take about an hour to play and is a good lock-in activity. Using non-public rooms after hours for the crime scenes makes it all the more mysterious and fun. Ask library staff to pose as the sheriffs for each team for interaction with the teens.

Six teens will play on a team and each team should have an adult sheriff with them. The adult will guide the suspects to the correct rooms and keep order to the questioning. It helps to color code the teams, sheriffs, and playing pieces, so you have a red team, a blue team, and so on. Each team will be solving the crime independently, so there will be a different solution and a winner (and guilty suspect) for each one.

The first step is deciding on a theme for the game. The Summer Reading Program theme for the year I made this game had a Medieval theme so I used a castle theme for the game and called it Castle Clue. I will use Castle Clue to explain the game in detail, but it can be easily adapted to many other themes, including space, international, and circus. The game is planned for six teens on each team. Adjust the number of characters to the number of teens you will have on a team.

1. Create six suspects, six weapons, and six rooms for the crime:

Suspects:	Weapons:	Rooms:
Scullery Maid	Battle Ax	Dungeon
Dungeon Master	Dagger	The Keep
Gate Keeper	Crossbow	Tower
Knight Errant	Mace	Moat
Peasant	Halberd	Battlements
Wandering Minstrel	Sword	Gatehouse

2. Write a scenario. In a word processing or publishing program, orient the paper to landscape, divide it into four columns and copy the scenario into each column, add a frame around each column, print enough copies for one column for each player and cut apart:

Court Jester Fools Around Once Too Often!

Most assuredly no one died of laughter at last evening's feast. The court jester apparently had an off night as his body has been found in the castle! The Lord of the castle has demanded that all the suspects of this heinous crime (all seen heckling the jester during his performance) be taken to the possible crime scenes, and the sheriff will listen to each of them ask questions to absolve themselves of suspicion. You are a suspect! You must try to discover who did it? Where did he or she do it? And what weapon was used? Ask your questions carefully, the other suspects are listening for clues! No one wants to be LOCKED IN the dungeon!

3. Write a clue list of suspects, weapons, and rooms. Using the landscape orientation and four columns on a page set up on the word processor, type the list of suspects, leave a few spaces, type the list of weapons, leave a few spaces, and type the list of rooms in a single column. Add a frame, copy, and paste the form to the other columns. Print enough for one column for each player and cut apart. Each player will use this list to gather clues. These will look similar to the playing sheets in the Clue® board game.

4. Make playing cards on the word processor using portrait orientation. Divide a page into three columns and six rows. Type each suspect, weapon, and room, one in each square. Print out one copy on a different colored sheet of paper for each team. Cut apart. You will now have a full set of playing cards in each team's color.

5. Make clue notebooks with plain corrugated cardboard cut from boxes into 8" x 10" rectangles. Cut down the center long ways through one paper side of the cardboard rectangle so it can be folded in half neatly. An Exacto knife and ruler make this job quick and neat. A copy of the scenario is glued to the front. On the inside, glue the list of suspects, weapons, and rooms to the right side and half a coin envelope on the left for carrying the playing cards. Number each notebook on the back, 1–6.

6. Create the weapons from cardboard and aluminum foil and wooden dowels. Pictures may be found on the Internet or in books if you need a pattern. Teen volunteers or the TAB can help make the weapons unless you want it to be a surprise. Realism isn't necessary so add a bit of comedy with cartoon looking weapons.

7. Make suspect name tags and sheriff stars, one set for each team, color coded to the playing cards. Leave room for players to write their real names under the character names.

8. To set up the crime scenes, an outline of the jester's body was made in each of the rooms. Staff volunteered to be jester bodies and laid down on the floor so I could make body outlines using masking tape, adding the shape of pointed shoes and a hat to each outline. The obvious fact that the body outlines were of entirely different people added a bit of humor. A jester hat made from paper was placed near each body outline with a jester prop: juggling balls, magic flowers, a scarf, playing cards, or coins. A sign and props in each room designated which crime scene they were visiting. The scenes were set as follows: The dungeon had paper chains hanging on the wall, a skeleton borrowed from Hal-

Figure 6–3 Live Clue Notebooks.
**Each player receives a notebook to collect clues. The front has a copy
of the scenario, the inside has the playing cards and clue list.**

loween decorations, and dim lighting which set this scene located in a
book sale storage room that we really do call the dungeon! The keep
was simply a cloth spread on a table with a wooden bowl of bread and
fruit, a candelabra, and low lighting. This scene was placed in the center of a large dark basement room. The tower was perfectly set at the
top of a secret spiral staircase closed to the public. The moat was outside the dock doors in the bookmobile garage. The moat was created
with a large sheet of blue paper. A green paper alligator lurked just below the surface and a jester hat floated nearby. All that remained of the
jester was his gloved hand (a water filled latex glove)! There was no body
outline. A staff member hid in the garage with a Super Shooter water
gun and squirted whoever peeked in to look into the moat. The pages'
room leads to the docking doors opening to the moat, so it was a perfect location for the gatehouse. The battlements were in the staff room,

which is the highest room in the building. Gargoyles and a stockpile of weapons we had borrowed from collectors and the museum set the scene. The items had been used for displays in the library during the medieval summer reading program. The teens weren't able to touch these items, but they were very effective for setting the scene.

Figure 6–4 Jester Crime Scene.
Every crime leaves some clues! Each vignette had a jester body outline and some props. This scene was the Gatehouse. The doors opened into the moat where an accomplice lay in wait with a super soaker water gun!

Figure 6–5 Live Clue Team.
One of these suspects will be found out! Each team has a guilty culprit.

How to play the game:

The object of the game is to deduce who the guilty suspect is on the team, what weapon was used, and in what room the crime was committed by eliminating clues. Each player receives a clue notebook, a name tag with a character's name, and a pencil. The story is read aloud to the whole group to introduce the game. Each sheriff has the 18 clue cards for his team. He secretly chooses one weapon card, one suspect card, and one room card, and hides them in a pocket before the game begins. Those cards are the solutions for his team. The remaining cards are passed out to his team as evenly as possible. The teens cross the clues they hold off their lists, place their clue cards in the card pockets in their notebooks, and they are ready to go to the first room.

To avoid congestion and confusion, send each team to a different room to begin the game and they proceed to the next room in the order the rooms appear on their clue cards. The sheriff is responsible for getting the team to the right room, and deciding who goes first. The simplest method is asking the suspects to stand in the order they appear on the clue sheet in their notebooks and in the first room, the first suspect takes the first turn, in the second, the second suspect, and so on. The numbers on the back of their clue notebooks will help the sheriff to keep them in order.

A player takes a turn by turning to the suspect next to him and making a guess. Example: "I think the Scullery Maid did it with the Battle Ax in the Dungeon." That suspect would then look through his own clue cards, show only that player—the Scullery Maid or the Battle Ax or the Dungeon card. If he has none of them, the player asks the next suspect until one player can show him one card. He can then mark that clue off his list and the next player gets to play. The players are supposed to keep their suspicions secret and not show their cards to anyone but the player asking the question, but some collaboration usually takes place! Each player gets one turn to ask a question in each room. He should listen to the other players' questions and observe if cards are shown and compare with his own clue list.

When a player thinks he has a solution, he makes an official announcement to the sheriff and then makes his best guess. If any of the players can show a card to prove him wrong, his turns are over but he must remain with the group to be asked questions by the other players. If his solution is correct, he wins for that team.

When all the teams have finished, we meet in the meeting room where winners and guilty suspects are announced. I give small prizes to the winner and to the guilty suspect of each team.

THE BOTTOM LINE

Dungeons and Dragons players provide their own books and game pieces. I provide a bag of cookies or chips and a two-liter bottle of soda. The only expenses for Castle Clue were the small prizes, which can be as simple as a bag of candy the winner may choose to share with his team. All the props were borrowed or made with supplies on hand. Extra adult help is needed, so play this game as the opening activity at a lock-in so the extra staff or volunteers can leave when you are finished. Purchased mystery games vary in price, averaging $50.00 to $75.00.

THE COLLECTION CONNECTION

For the Castle Clue, books on castles, medieval weapons, and knights. The game was also good for exploring the behind the scenes areas in the library, and staff members who were sheriffs got the opportunity to interact with the teens. Books on the theme can be displayed at each crime scene. Use your imagination and your teens' when deciding on a theme for this game. The teens can help set the scenes and make the weapons since it won't affect their playing the game. A space theme would be lots of fun if you created a Star Wars scene, a Star Trek scene, a Jetsons scene, a Battlestar Galactica scene, a Lost in Space scene, or a Buck Rogers scene. If a murder mystery—no matter how comical—is too grisly sounding for your community, try using a different mysterious event. A library mascot (the director?!) could be missing!

GAME SHOW PROGRAMS

Survive Jeopardy and Feel Like a Millionaire

Survive Jeopardy and Feel Like a Millionaire was a twist on several TV game shows. Our game was combined with a Pizza Taste-Off for our Teen Read Week program on a Thursday evening from 7 p.m.–8:30 p.m. Our intrepid director agreed to be Vanna Anna and a friend was the game show host, Rob Mybanks. The questions were displayed on a wall in six categories, Jeopardy style, but were written as questions with multiple choice answers like Who Wants to Be a Millionaire. The questions were in pocket folders hanging underneath the posted categories. The contestant selected a category and Vanna Anna chose a question randomly from the pocket folder. Each question with the multiple-choice answers was printed out as large as would fit it on a single sheet of paper. This worked well, as the contestant could read it easily and the game show host read it aloud to the audience as Vanna Anna displayed it in a spokesmodel style. Each contestant could answer up to three questions correctly and win a prize for each question. He could use a lifeline (poll the audience) once during his turn. Once a question was answered incorrectly, his turn was over. Prizes for correct answers were gift certificates donated from area fast food restaurants awarded with fanfare and applause and there was a Bucket O' Lovely Parting Gifts for wrong answers (wax lips, Hal-

Figure 6–6 Survive Jeopardy and Feel Like a Millionaire Program. Vanna Anna does her spokesmodel pose while Rob Mybanks reads the question aloud in Survive Jeopardy and Feel Like a Millionaire.

loween makeup, pencils, temporary tattoos) so every player got a prize. An applause sign held up by Rob kept the audience involved.

Couch Potato
1. What is the name of Ally McBeal's law firm? *Cage/Fish & Associates*
2. What is Mike Brady's job? *Architect*
3. Bob Vila is Tim Taylor's long-standing arch-rival on what TV show? *Home Improvement*
4. A Times/CNN poll in June 1997 revealed that what percentage of Americans believe aliens from outer space have been in contact with humans at some point? *22 percent of Americans believe aliens have been in contact with humans. 13 percent of respondents also believed that aliens have abducted humans for observations or to perform experiments.*
5. What happens to Kenny every time after he dies? *Rats swarm over him*
6. What is the first name of the character Kramer on Seinfield? *Cosmo*
7. On the Simpsons, who did Krusty the Clown supposedly kill? *Mr. Burns*
8. What video game has a secret code to become the Beastie Boys? *NBA JAM*
9. Who sings the "Friends" theme song, "I'll Be There For You"? *The Rembrandts*
10. What did the original cast members of SNL call their troupe? *The Not Ready for Prime Time Players*
11. Who was the youngest person to ever host SNL? *Drew Barrymore*
12. Britney Spears got her show biz start on what TV show? *Star Search*

Figure 6–7 Couch Potato TV Trivia Questions.
This category featured TV trivia questions and answers.

Take Time to Read
1. How old do you have to be to use the Internet at the library without your parent's signature? *13*
2. What is this year's Teen Read Week slogan?? *Take Time to Read*
3. What does YA mean? *Young Adult*
4. How many lines are there in a sonnet? *14*
5. I Know What You Did Last Summer: who wrote the novel that the movie is based on? *Lois Duncan*
6. What is the best selling American book of all time? *Noah Webster's Blue-Backed Speller of 1783, revised and reprinted (over 100 million copies and still in print) is the all time best seller.*
7. Which fictional character has a weekly allowance of $100,000? *Ritchie Rich*
8. The word "nerd" was first coined by whom? *Dr. Seuss*
9. In Harry Potter and the Sorcerer's Stone who is the cat sitting on the wall? *Professor McGonagall*
10. Who is the most published American author of all time? *Mark Twain (1835-1910)*
11. Who is the reference librarian that will help you find information for a research paper? *RoseMary*
12. What is TRW, celebrated in October? *Teen Read Week*
13. When the librarian cards you at the library, she is: *Going to check out your books, comics, magazines, CD Roms, CDs, or tapes*

Figure 6–8 Take Time to Read Library/Book Trivia Questions.
This category featured library and book trivia questions and answers.

Let's Get Ready to Rumble
1. A perfect bowling game has how many strikes? *12*
2. Who owns the World Wrestling Federation? *Vince McMahon*
3. Who was the last torch bearer to light the Olympic Flame at the 2000 Olympics? *Cathy Freeman*
4. Which sporting event is new to this Olympics? *Triathlon*
5. If you wanted to find a book about Tiger Woods, you would: *Search for "Woods, Tiger" under the subject search on the Dynix catalog. OR Ask RoseMary to help you find it*
6. Which Tribe player was in the Final Four? *Kenny Lofton*
7. Who wears number 13? *Omar Vizquel*
8. What is the left-field wall at Jacob's Field called? *Jacob's Ladder*
9. How many Olympic gold medals did Mark Spitz win? *9. Swimmer Mark Spitz won 7 gold medals in the 1972 world Olympics, a record for the highest number of gold medals won by an individual in a single Olympics. He also won 2 gold medals in the 1968 games in Mexico City.*
10. Austin feuded with this man, who was his boss, in many epic battles: *Vince McMahon*

Figure 6–9 Get Ready to Rumble Sports Trivia Questions.
This category featured sports trivia questions and answers.

Want Fries With That?

1. How much cheese does the average American eat in one year? *23 pounds*
2. How many times per year does the average family eat pizza? *30*
3. In what country has McDonald's served McSpaghetti? *Philippines*
4. In which country are Big Macs made without "all beef" patties? *India, the "Maharaja Mac" is made with lamb.*
5. How many ingredients are on a Big Mac? *7 — two all-beef patties, special sauce, lettuce, cheese, pickles, onions on a sesame seed bun.*
6. Which of the following fast food chains was founded first in America? *White Castle, which was founded in 1921 in Wichita, Kansas. McDonald's was founded in 1955 in Des Plaines, Illinois; Burger King, in 1954 in Miami, Florida; and Dairy Queen, in 1940 in Joliet, Illinois.*
7. What year was Diet Coke invented? *1982*
8. Is each different colored piece of Froot Loops® cereal a different flavor? *No*
9. What was the original name of "Dr Pepper"? *"Shoot a Waco"*
10. At current rates, about how long does it take to sell a billion gallons of Coca-Cola worldwide? *Seven months*
11. According to the Guinness Book of World Records, the world's largest popcorn ball weighed. . . . *Weighed 2,000 pounds and was 12 feet in diameter*
12. What is the average number of licks it takes to polish off a single scoop ice cream cone? *50*

Figure 6–10 Want Fries With That? Fast Food Trivia Questions.
This category featured fast food trivia questions and answers.

Two Thumbs Up

1. George Lucas's original 13-page story treatment for *Star Wars* — set initially in the twenty-third century — purported to tell the story of what character, now a prominent figure in *The Phantom Menace*? *Mace Windu (Samuel L. Jackson). That now famous early draft posited a film chronicling, "the story of Mace Windu, a revered Jedi-bendu of Opuchi who was related to Usby C.J. Thape, padawan learner of the famed Jedi."*
2. What is the name of Bond's CIA counterpart? *Felix Leiter*
3. In the *Blues Brothers*, what does Jake order at the diner? *Four fried chickens and a coke*
4. Who are producers trying to get to star in the *Matrix* sequel? *Jet Li*
5. In *Jurassic Park*: What does Dennis Nedry use to transport the stolen embryos? *A can of shaving cream*
6. What year saw the release of the first *Karate Kid*? *1984*
7. What was the name of the plantation in *Gone with the Wind*? *Tara*
8. Who was the voice of Mr. Potato Head in the movie *Toy Story*? *Don Rickles*
9. How old was Rose DeWitt Bukater in the movie *Titanic*? *17*
10. *I Know What You Did Last Summer*: what does the killer use to kill people? *A hook*

Figure 6–11 Two Thumbs Up Movie Trivia Questions.
This category featured movie trivia questions and answers.

Trick or Treat
1. Every Halloween, Charlie Brown helps his friend Linus wait for what character to appear? *The Great Pumpkin*
2. Which country celebrates "The Day of the Dead" instead of Halloween? *Mexico*
3. What are male witches called? *Warlocks*
4. What is the name of the serial killer in the film *Halloween*? *Michael Myers*
5. What "phobia" do you suffer from if you have an intense fear of Halloween? *Samhainophobia*
6. Many of Stephen King's horror stories take place in this New England town. *Castle Rock*
7. Which of the following names are a witch's: Typhoid Mary, Jean Grenier, or Sarah Good? *Sarah Good was one of the Salem witches*
8. The tradition of dressing up started because: *We try to scare away evil spirits.*
9. Who first celebrated what we've come to know as Halloween? *The Druids*
10. Halloween is celebrated on the eve of what Christian holiday? *All Saints Day*

Figure 6–12 Trick or Treat Halloween Trivia Questions.
This category featured Halloween trivia questions and answers.

I Can Name That Tune in Three Notes

1. At what concert was the band 98° discovered? *Boys II Men*
2. What act holds the record for most #1 hits? *The Beatles*
3. What was the first rap song to ever hit #1? *"Ice Ice Baby" by Vanilla Ice*
4. Which rock singer started out in life as plain old Gordon Sumner? *Sting*
5. What is the first name of the lead singer of SmashMouth? *Steve*
6. What was the name of Paul McCartney's first band? *The Quarrymen was McCartney's first band. John Lennon formed the band, named after his high school (Quarry Bank), in 1957. McCartney joined in 1959. The Quarrymen's lineup changed numerous times, becoming the Beatles in 1960.*
7. Who was the first rock star to be arrested on stage? *Jim Morrison*
8. Believe it or not, Mr. Yankovic's first name isn't "Weird." It's actually Al, but what is Al short for? *Alfred, "Weird Al"'s full name is Alfred Matthew Yankovic.*
9. Which of the following fairy tale movies did Canadian rocker Brian Adams NOT supply a song for: "Robin Hood: Prince of Thieves," "Ever After: A Cinderella Story," or "The Three Musketeers?" *Adams did not supply a tune for 1998's "Ever After," but he did provide the love song "Everything I Do" (I do it for you) for 1991's "Robin Hood: Prince of Thieves" and teamed up with Sting and Rod Stewart for Musketeers' theme "All For Love."*
10. Many comics made their way to Broadway. Which strip gave us a show that in turn gave us such songs as "It's a Hard-Knock Life" and "Tomorrow"? *Annie*
11. On February 9, 1964, this band got $2,400 to play The Ed Sullivan Show. They must not have improved much, because on April 24, 1978, Saturday Night Live producer Lorne Michaels offered them a mere $3,000 to perform live for his show. Which band was this? *The Beatles*
12. How many Grammy's has Babyface won? *10*

Figure 6–13 Name That Tune Music Trivia Questions.
This category featured music trivia questions and answers.

Whose Line Is It Anyway?

For a Teen Read Week program, we had a game show modeled after the TV program Whose Line Is It Anyway? The TV show is popular with teens and adults and is a great opportunity to give teens a chance to ham it up and try out their improv talents. The program was held on a Thursday evening from 7 p.m.–8:30 p.m.

The games used on the TV show are listed on the Internet. They were printed and passed around at a Teen Advisory Board meeting and the teens were asked to choose their favorites. The names of the games, party quirks, and date quirks were written on pieces of paper for the host to choose for the players. Props were collected for the home shopping and props games. As the teens arrived and signed in, they were asked to write phrases for the Whose Line game and ideas for Scenes From a Hat. A buzzer from a Taboo® game was available for the host to signal when a game was over.

The room was set up like a coffeehouse in a semicircle around a stage area with four chairs. I decorated with red, white, and blue balloons, and table covers to recognize the teens' patriotism during the aftermath of September 11th. Books from the YA room about acting, auditions, monologues, comedy, and improv were available for browsing on the tables. Chips, trail mix, cookies, soda, cocoa, and cappuccino were all self-serve refreshments.

I acted as the first host. Three young people with theater experience helped me start the program with the Questions Only game (two players may communicate with questions only, the host buzzes out the player who fails to ask a question and the other player jumps in to continue) and Sports Commentators (two players give a play-by-play report of another player putting together Mr. Potato Head in slow motion). After these two skits, I then called up four teens for Let's Make a Date and gave the three contestants date quirks for answering their questions. The object is for the bachelorette/bachelor to guess what the quirk is for each potential date after they have answered questions in their character. When the teens saw how the games would work, I picked a teen to be the next host and we continued to changed hosts every two to three skits throughout the evening. Each host chose players, which skit for them to do, and any quirks or props for them to use and also decided when the game was over by pressing the buzzer. All participants chose a prize from treat bags on the host desk each time they played a game. The small prizes included trading cards, nail polish, sports magnets, and lip gloss.

BOARD GAMES

Monopoly® Tournament

The Monopoly® Tournament has been a summer tradition at our library for six years. This is an event that always attracts more boys than girls. Play-

Figure 6–14 Let's Make a Date.
Four contestants play Let's Make a Date at the Whose Line improv program. Each potential date has a quirk or trait and answers his questions accordingly. The questioner has to determine what those quirks and traits are by their answers.

ers are required to pre-register so I know how many bankers to ask to help, how many tables to set up, and how much food to buy. Hasbro requires 24 players to make an official tournament. The room is set up with a table and five chairs for each game of four players with a banker. The tables are numbered with a tent card and an unopened Monopoly® game is placed on each. A table at one end of the room is reserved for food.

Our tournament is held on a Saturday and we open the door at 9 a.m. The first half-hour is spent getting players registered and bankers assigned to tables, getting some juice and donuts, and reviewing the official tournament rules. After the teens sign in, they draw a number to decide which table is theirs. Each player and banker has a set of rules to refer to. I am the referee and co-workers and friends volunteer to be bankers. A banker oversees each game and does not play and the referee is there to settle disputes or clarify the rules and watch the time.

Ten minutes before play the bankers count out the money and the boards are set up. The first round of play is timed for 90 minutes. Scores are tabulated over a pizza lunch and the finalists announced. The six finalists play a second 90-minute round in the afternoon. Many of the teens stay for the whole day to see who wins and to play more Monopoly® or other games and have snacks.

Hasbro (phone 413–525–6411) will send forms, score sheets, tournament rules, and games for your tournament. They also include a variety of other games (Boggle®, Stratego®) you can use for prizes. In an official tournament, the grand champion's score sheet is notarized and sent to Hasbro with a photo of the winner for the national competition.

Figure 6–15 Monopoly® Tournament.
Serious real estate transactions take place under the watchful eye of the banker.

THE BOTTOM LINE

The Monopoly® games are free from Hasbro and you can use the other free games as prizes. The Friends of the Library pay for the food at our tournaments, but you may be able to get donated or discounted pizzas; ask the Teen Advisory Board to bring bags of snacks or skip the juice and donuts to save money. The first year we saved the Monopoly® games and gave the other free games for prizes. Every year since then, we have used those same Monopoly® games for the tournament play and have given the six finalists the six new Monopoly® games. I saved the other free games for the rest of the teens to play in the afternoon and for other board game programs and the lock-ins. The Friends also give the grand champion $50 in Coshocton County Bucks, which are gift certificates that can be used in many local businesses. Award the first bankrupt player with a Pay Day candy bar. It is always accepted with great fanfare!

Board Game Nights, Chess, Scrabble®

Game Nights can be offered as an after-school program or part of summer reading. During the Medieval summer we held five chess nights for all ages. Players brought their own chess sets. Any board games you can round up makes a fun social time for teens. Always include snacks, but they don't have to be fancy: popcorn, chips, or cookies, and soda will do fine. Background music is nice to have for quiet games.

We have also held Scrabble® tournaments. Players bring their own Scrabble® games and a King of the Hill Tournament is played. This involves two timed rounds. The players sit at any table for the first round. After the scores are totaled, the players are placed at tables from high to low scores. The four highest scoring players will play each other, the second highest group of four play each other and so on. The King of the Hill is the player with the highest total points from both games. A small prize is awarded to the King of the Hill.

THE BOTTOM LINE

Prizes and food are your main expense for game programs. Borrow the games and add a few to your collection each year or ask players to bring their own. Coupons for free food from fast food and pizza restaurants are favorite prizes.

THE COLLECTION CONNECTION

Gear the questions towards your theme, library, or materials in the game shows, ask other librarians to play the host and Vanna parts in a game show or act as bankers in Monopoly® so the teens get a chance to interact with them. Have commercial breaks during game show programs to advertise teen materials, services, and upcoming programs.

TEEN FEEDBACK

- "The Role Playing Club we have is the best thing to do here on Thursdays. We have fun with friends and just have a great time." Marc Garcia
- "My favorite is the Role Playing Game Night. I like D&D." Adam Richcreek

- "Whose Line Is It Anyway was the funniest program I've ever been a part of." Matt Shroyer
- "I really enjoyed Whose Line Is It Anyway. It was very funny and everyone was allowed to act." Javad Azadi
- "A program that I really enjoyed at the Coshocton Public Library is the Whose Line Is It Anyway improv. It was very enjoyable because I am a huge fan of the show and the prospect of trying to do some improvising myself really appealed to me because whenever I watch the show I always want to try doing it myself. Without the library and RoseMary, my dream to try improvising would never come true." Dustin Baker

RESOURCES

Barman, Julie. *Whose Page Is It Anyway* [Online]. Available: www.geocities.com/Hollywood/2549/wlgames.html [2002, May 11].

Bedford, Dean. *Whose Line is it Anyway Games Page* [Online]. Available: www.angelfire.com/tv2/deansline/games.html [2002, May 11].

Double Dog Press [Online]. Available: www.dbldog.com/ [2002, May 11].

Teen Mystery Games [Online]. Available: www.djmcadam.com/teen-mystery.html [2002, May 11].

Whodunnit Mystery Games [Online]. Available: www.whodunnitmysteries.com/ [2002, May 11].

Chapter 7

Coffeehouse Programs

OVERVIEW

Coffeehouses provide a relaxed and comfortable atmosphere for showcasing teen talents. If your community has a coffee shop, consider arranging a program in the shop with the owner. Such an arrangement could be mutually beneficial. You would save money, energy, and time in creating the atmosphere and the coffee shop would have a busy profitable evening. However, a meeting room or classroom can be transformed into a coffeehouse with a little imagination and very little expense and some help from your teens. Several kinds of performance art programs can be held in a coffeehouse setting. This chapter describes a poetry program, a music program, and an open mike program. A similar setting was used for the Whose Line Is It Anyway? game program.

A COLLECTION OF COFFEEHOUSE PROGRAMS

Poetry Night

A poetry night promotes poetry reading and writing among teens and gives teen poets an audience. Our poetry night is held on a Thursday evening during April to celebrate National Poetry Month and National Library Week. Teachers may offer extra credit for reading or the poetry night may qualify as a cultural event requirement in English classes. Asking them to consider doing so will encourage more teens to attend who may not have considered a poetry night to be cool or fun . . . until they get there!

To publicize our poetry night, posters, letters, and masters for bookmarks were sent to the English teachers in the schools, and bookmarks and posters were placed throughout the library, too. Members of the teen board wrote and read ads about the program on the school announcements. If you are holding the poetry night in a local coffee shop, advertise there as well. Our publicity invited teens to read their own original poetry or a favorite poem.

To create a coffeehouse atmosphere in the meeting room, set up card tables borrowed from staff and teen board members. Our library has since purchased a number of small square tables for these events. A teacher who has used this idea in her classroom moved four desks together in a square to create the tables. Cover the tables with tan Kraft paper and add a coffee mug of markers for doodling and poetry writing. A jar candle or battery candle in the center of the table adds ambiance. Other simple ideas to embellish the coffee shop tables are menus listing the beverages, a poetry book or two, paper napkins, and library pencil favors.

Figure 7–1 Poetry Night Table.
Set up the tables for coffeehouse fun: graffiti, poetry reading, poetry games, beverages, and snacks.

The table art the teens create at our poetry nights is too interesting to throw away. I cut around the artwork and apply it to the counter in the YA room with clear contact paper and add a label explaining it was art from Teen Poetry Night. This has sparked more interest in the next program from other teens. Following years I have made collage posters of the artwork to use in the YA room to promote the program.

ALA Celebrity READ posters make decorating the walls a simple task. The posters can be used as door prizes at the end of the program or framed with poster frames for the YA room. A Teen Board member knew where she could borrow a black photographer's curtain so we used it for the backdrop of the stage area, but any dark drapery or rolls of dark paper would work. A borrowed kitchen stool with a red beret sitting on it is placed center stage. A banner made on MSPublisher attached to the curtain announced it was "Teen Poetry Night."

A portable display board set up on a table shows Internet sites where teen poetry can be published. Library books, handouts, and bookmarks about writing and publishing poetry are arranged on the table for browsing. Famous lines of poetry can be printed in fancy script fonts and posted on the walls.

Play jazz music CDs as teens arrive and during restroom and beverage breaks. A high school band member can play a set of bongos to add to the beatnik coffeehouse atmosphere or you might invite a guitarist to play. Some

Figure 7–2 Poetry Night Teen Poets.
These two poets presented "Star Wars in 30 Seconds"—a "very"
original work complete with sound effects and character voices.

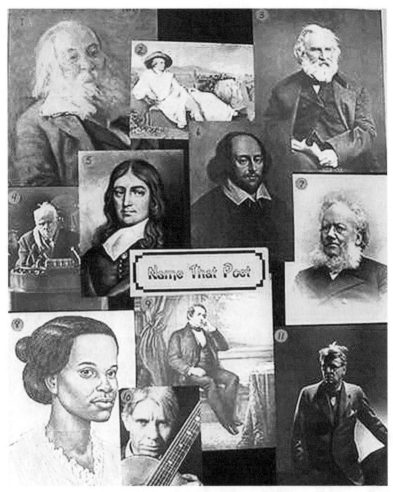

Figure 7–3 Poetry Night Name That Poet Poster.
Can the teens identify the faces of the famous poets they learn about in school?

of the teen board members came dressed in black and wearing shades. Finger snapping applause followed each reading.

As a variation of the popular magnetic poetry sets, a poetry board can be created with a sheet of plywood covered with carpet and bound with heavy tape. This makes a portable but sturdy board to use at the program and to move into the YA room afterwards. The poetry board has had some thoughtful poems and also some funny phrases on it and was a fun activity at the program. A temporary lightweight board could be constructed from cardboard and flannel. Instructions for making a poetry board are in the independent program chapter.

Another independent game, Name That Poet, was posted on a wall with a drawing box and was available for teens to play before the poetry reading began and during breaks. To make the game, I gathered portraits of classical poets and mounted them in a collage on a poster. I had saved portraits from the vertical file but you can also download them from the Internet or scan them from books. Each picture is numbered. The answer form has the name of each poet and a blank before each name to write the number of the portrait. The object of the game is to match the face with the name. The teens exchanged forms for "grading" during a break in the poetry reading and I handed out coffee mug prizes for the most correct answers.

---

  1. Walt Whitman
  2. Johann Wolfgang Goethe
  3. Henry Wadsworth Longfellow
  4. Robert Frost
  5. John Milton
  6. William Shakespeare
  7. Henrik Ibsen
  8. Phyllis Wheatley
  9. Washington Irving
 10. Carl Sandburg
 11. William Butler Yeats

**Figure 7–4 Poetry Night Name That Poet Answer Sheet.
Can you Name That Poet?? Here are the answers!**

The refreshments at the coffeehouse can be self-serve. Provide individual packets of cappuccino, flavored coffee, and cocoa in a basket and place by a big coffeemaker holding hot water. Whipped cream, flavored creamers, and marshmallows are fun trimmings. Sodas or other cold drinks should also be available. TAB members brought the snacks, which were cookies and home-made biscotti, but other homemade baked goods or pastries from the bakery would be great, too.

On coffeehouse night, the teens signed in on a numbered list including their names, high schools, and English teachers' names. This provided a record to notify the teachers with a list of the students that attended so extra credit could be awarded. They could make a beverage, look at the displays, play at the poetry board, play the Name That Poet game, and visit as others arrived.

When everyone was settled, I turned off the music and welcomed everyone. I explained I would be drawing numbers from a bowl that would coordinate with the numbers on the sign-in sheet. Whoever signed in on that numbered line would take their turn reading or reciting poetry. This way no one was "put on the spot" because everyone's turn was coming and there were no awkward silences waiting for a volunteer. No one was required to read, but more than half the teens usually do and much of it is original poetry. The audience was quiet and respectful of the readers and applauded generously with clapping and finger snapping for each poem. After everyone had read once, volunteers could read again. The numbers were thrown back into the bowl for the door prize drawing for the ALA posters at the end of the program.

The content of the poems ranged from funny to serious, thoughtful to silly. Some of the teens asked a friend to read for them, which gave them the opportunity to hear their own work and watch the audience's response. One teen read a poem her aunt had written for her the day she was born. A few of the teens wrote spontaneous poems on the table covers, tore them off and read them to the group. A few read favorites from Shel Silverstein and one teen recites "The Jabberwocky," his favorite poem, from memory every year.

GROUP POETRY GAMES

Poetry games and activities can be incorporated into the poetry night program. The Poetry Machine is a group effort to compose a poem. Make alphabet cards (one letter on each card) and pass around two or more to each player. Write the first line of a poem on a flip chart for all to see. The object of the game is for the teens at each table to work together to add a line to the poem using words that begin with the letters on their cards. After passing out the letters, give the teens a few minutes to make short lists of nouns, verbs, adjectives, and adverbs beginning with their letters (they can write them on the table covers). I had numbered the tables and drew numbers to decide which table went next so our game was very impromptu. You may add whatever rules you like for form and rhyme, adding free articles and conjunctions, etc. You can write the last line if you need to make the number of lines even. The teens considered it only fair that I had to come up with the last line. Our poem began "T'was Teen Poetry Night at the library . . ." and had to rhyme in couplets. Expect major silliness! Read the final poem aloud to the group. If you have a small group, go around the room twice.

Mad Libs is another fun group game to play at a coffeehouse. Write a familiar poem on a flip chart before the program, drawing blanks for nouns, verbs, adjectives, and adverbs. Write the part of speech that should fill in each blank right below the line. "The Road Not Taken" by Robert Frost and the first verse of "The Raven" by Edgar Allen Poe were our choices. Face the flipchart away from the audience and choose a teen to come up to write in the words as they are suggested by the players. To play, teens choose one of the letters on their table and when asked for a part of speech, his answer must begin with that letter. To call on players, you can draw their numbers or just go around the room.

A little creative writing exercise called Composition is always good for some laughs. Each table gets a sheet of paper and a paper clip. The first writer starts a story by writing two lines. He then folds the top edge of the paper over his words, fastens it with a paper clip, and then writes two words to begin the next line. The paper is then passed to the next writer at his table. That writer completes the sentence and adds another, folds it down, adds two words to start another line and passes it on. This continues as long as you want the game to last or until the page is full. Give a warning signal to finish the story. Each table chooses someone to read their story to the audience.

A game to play that will test their memories is a Poem Puzzle. Print out copies of a famous poem and cut the lines apart. The object is to reassemble lines in the correct order. We used "How Do I Love Thee?" by Elizabeth Barrett Browning. Most teens know the first two lines and the last, but maybe not the middle. You can make it a little easier by cutting the poem into couplets—that is two lines on each puzzle piece.

Music Revue/Karaoke

The Reading Rocks theme for Teen Read Week inspired a music program called The Reading Rocks Music Revue. The revue offered the teens an opportunity to perform instrumental or voice pieces or sing with a karaoke machine. A new YA CD collection was introduced during the program for the karaoke.

The meeting room was set up coffeehouse-style as described in the poetry night section. The centerpieces for the paper-covered card tables were black paper plates filled with Jelly Belly jelly beans and a jar candle in the center. A Jelly Belly menu (available at Jelly Belly display counters) stood on each table, music note confetti was sprinkled around, and black cocktail napkins and a coffee mug of markers finished the tables. Large music notes found at a party supply store hung from the ceiling. ALA Celebrity READ posters decorated the walls, but music group posters would be very popular if you are able to acquire them. Feature books on musicians, bands, how to play instruments, and sheet music on a display table and each card table. The books and CDs should be available for checkout at the end of the evening. The refreshments were self-serve cappuccino, cocoa, and soda provided by the Friends and the snacks were donated by the TAB.

My son-in-law Eric opened our Music Revue with a couple of humorous

ballads. He had played in bands in high school and college and his performance set an informal relaxed atmosphere. He brought his keyboard, acous-
tic guitar, a microphone, and amplifier, and offered assistance to the teens if
they wanted to use the equipment for their performances. Then the stage
was opened to the teens, who quickly volunteered to perform. Some had
brought music with them and many wanted to try the karaoke.

Figure 7–5 Music Revue Guest Musician.
**Eric, our guest musician, warms up the group with an amusing
ballad.**

The karaoke machine was rented for $30.00 at a local electronics store. It
could play the CDs normally or with the voice track turned off. The inserts
from the CDs had the lyrics printed in them so no other source was needed.
Solos and groups of teens sang along to the music of The Backstreet Boys,
N'Sync, and Britney Spears, to name a few. The evening closed with the whole
group gathered around the stage area. Eric led everyone in a sing along of
Weird Al's Star Wars song, "A Legend Begins."

To help publicize the Revue, an independent game, Unmask the Musicians, was posted in the YA room for two weeks prior to the program. The
display case featured the TAB and the year's programs with the title banner,

Figure 7–6 Music Revue Karaoke.
Look out Britney and Backstreet Boys, the Karaoke Krooners are on the scene!

Figure 7–7 Music Revue Closing Song.
"A Legend Begins" at the Music Revue! The teens gathered together for a closing number.

Teens Are A Hit At The Coshocton Public Library. New books about bands and musicians were on display. Letters were sent to the school band and choir directors to publicize the event to music students.

Open Mike Night

Poetry, skits, singing, karaoke, jokes, readings, pantomime, juggling, instrumentals, story telling—any of these talents can be part of a coffeehouse program. Set up a stage area and small tables arranged so everyone will be able to see. The decorations can go with any theme. Posters are the fastest way to decorate walls and make great door prizes. Markers and paper covered tables inspire creativity. Balloons and banners can make the room look festive for a party atmosphere. Refreshments are an important part of the coffeehouse.

THE BOTTOM LINE

The drinks and cups are provided by the Friends and cost about $30.00 for each coffeehouse. The TAB provides the snacks. If you have the funds or love to bake, fancy coffee shop pastries would be nice to add. I used ALA READ posters the library already owned for the first coffeehouse and have since purchased a few for each event. ALA posters are about $12.00 each, but an ALA membership will give you a discount. The coffee mug prizes and kraft paper table covers were from Naeir. The karaoke machine cost $30.00 to rent from a local electronics store.

THE COLLECTION CONNECTION

For poetry night display poetry, poets, National Library Week, National Poetry Month, how to write, how to get published, and Internet sites for teen writing. The Music Revue can launch a new music collection and feature books on bands, instruments, how to play, musicians, sheet music, performance. Use Open Mike Night to promote any performance art books and materials.

TEEN FEEDBACK

- "Teen Poetry Night is a great way to express yourself. Even if you don't feel like reading your own or another author's poetry, drawing on the tablecloths and the mood in general is well worth your time." Amy Schlegel
- A teacher called me the afternoon following our first poetry night. He said his class was so excited and chatty about the program that he wasn't able to administer a test. I think I made a few friends in that class!

RESOURCES

The Academy of American Poets [Online]. Available: www.poets.org/ [2002, May 11].

Honnold, RoseMary. 2001. "Reading Rocks Music Revue." *VOYA* (October): 257.

Jones, Jeanne G. 1998. "No Holds Barred at the Teen Poetry Coffeehouse." *VOYA* (April): 19.

Chapter 8

Scavenger Hunts

OVERVIEW

Scavenger hunts are great ways for teens to learn about the library and how to do fast and efficient catalog searches. They also provide the physical activity teens need and want. The Space Mission and Library Survivor are samples of hunts suited to after-hour lock-ins or parties as there will be laughter and silliness involved and they take some preparation! The teens will have opportunity for teamwork and creativity. It is helpful to have an adult in each area of the library where the teens will be hunting to provide assistance and supervision. Pre-registration can help you plan the activities for these programs.

The Library Tour is a shorter hunt and can be used at the spur of the moment with a class visit and the teens may work together or individually. Sandy Marvin, high school librarian at Coshocton High School, uses scavenger hunts so students may practice their research skills. She awards one prize each day of the hunt to the student who submits the most correct entries. You may have general questions about the library for the hunt or specific trivia questions if you want the students to explore certain resources. A hunt on the online catalog or on the Internet would be a fun way to teach searching skills. An explanation of the steps the player took to find the answer should be required as part of the answer.

You need about ten searches and activities for an hour to an hour and a half long lock-in hunt. Using these hunts as models, you can create your own using any summer reading theme or research theme. The ten tasks should involve finding something in the library using a research skill or discovering services and materials the teens may not have known were available. Once they accomplish a library skill, such as a catalog search, there is a fun activity to do that is connected (no matter how remotely) to the topic they searched. To plan a scavenger hunt, start with an idea for a theme. Make a list of ten topics related to the theme. Use those topics to plan the book and materials searches. Then plan an activity related to each search. The activities usually depend upon the props and equipment I find during the planning stages. Sudden inspiration can occur when spotting a fishing net in the sports department of a store!

O, Librarian! Where Art Thou: A Library Odyssey is an example of a hunt that is in the planning stages now. The hunt will be loosely based on the movie "O Brother! Where Art Thou?," which is loosely based on *The Odyssey* by Homer. Possible topics for the searches might be: epic poetry, camping skills, wild game cookery, folk music, the Depression, flooding of the Tennessee Valley, hair styles, and Greek history. The Tennessee Valley calls for a water game, they will have to wear hair nets to be a Dapper Dan man like the Ulysses character, the online catalogs will be the Oracle that gives them signs to show the way. There will be a Cyclops and an elusive treasure. More ideas will evolve as props are discovered in closets and basements!

We Have a Mission! and Library Survivor are fully described below so you can see how the theme, searches, and activities evolve into a hunt. You may use envelopes that are color coded with stickers for each team at each catalog station so the instructions aren't carried off with the first team. A library used the Mission scavenger hunt with over 40 teens. They made a map of the library for each team that showed where each task was located. The instructions were posted at each site and the teams were given ten minutes to complete an activity and then rotated. That method would save some preparation time and confusion with a large group.

A COLLECTION OF SCAVENGER HUNTS

We Have a Mission! A Space Theme Scavenger Hunt

This hunt was used as an opening activity for a teen lock-in at the close of a space theme Summer Reading Program and lasted one hour and fifteen minutes. The instructions in italics describe what needs to be prepared ahead of time and put in place before the hunt begins. The teens are assembled together in the meeting room and each team is given the "We Have a Mission" scenario with book bag that contains a lab coat and a colored dot to wear on the forehead for each teen. Read the scenario aloud as the coats and dots (a different color for each team) are given out and let each team leave the room a few minutes apart when they are dressed and ready.

A spaceship has landed!
Our visitors from Mars arrived safely but unfortunately
can't do the research they planned because they
can't breathe our atmosphere! So they came to our
library (they are smart but not good researchers) and
asked if we could help them gather information about
Earth to take back home. So you will look
professional doing our research, you all need to wear
lab coats. You will also need to wear the colored dots
on your foreheads because we humans all look alike
to Martians! When you have your uniform on,
proceed to the first card catalog by the main entrance
on the main floor of the library. Take your bag with
you to collect your findings.

1. *Color coded envelopes with instructions for each team are waiting by the catalogs:*
   Safety First
   For your own safety, you need to construct and wear a safety helmet to protect you from the radiation from the spaceship during our research. *Basic Metallurgy* by Donald V. Brown may give us some guidance on what materials to use! Check out the shelves where you would find this book for further instructions.
   A few rolls of aluminum foil are placed on that shelf.
   It turns out that the best reflector for Martian space ship radiation is ALUMINUM FOIL. Construct and wear a helmet for protection and then go to the computer catalog by the local history room.

2. *Color-coded envelopes with instructions for each team are waiting at the catalog terminal.*
   Talk to Me
   Find this book on the shelf: *Mother Tongue: How Humans Create Language* using the online catalog computer.
   Place a couple boxes of paper clips by the book on the shelf.
   Amazing as it may seem, our paperclips have the exact configuration used in building a Martian Universal Translator bracelet! Assemble and wear one to be able to understand the rest of the instructions! Then proceed to the first card catalog by the main entrance.

3. *Color-coded envelopes with instructions for each team are waiting at the catalog terminal.*
   All Dressed Up and No Place to Go

Find the series *Peoples of the World* using the online catalog computer. *A color-coded envelope for each team with the following instructions is waiting by the books on the shelf. At the end of the aisle on a library table are materials for making the dolls—paper, scissors, crayons, pencils, and yes, the kids loved doing this!*

The Martians are curious about the different types of clothing earthlings wear. Make a paper doll complete with removable paper doll clothing that shows the traditional clothing for any one country featured in one of these books. Find the materials on the table at the end of the aisle and take your book with you. Then proceed to the YA room.

4. *An adult staff member with a Polaroid camera is waiting in the YA room to take their pictures.*

   Smile (or not), You're on Alien Camera!

   Our visitors need to understand our facial and body expressions to understand our language better. Our ambassador will take your team's picture. Each member of the team needs to show a DIFFERENT emotion in the same picture (happy, sad, surprised, angry, confused). When finished, take your picture with you and proceed to the last table at the south end of the library.

5. *Color-coded envelopes with instructions for each team and a couple city maps, paper, and pencils are placed on the table.*

   Wash Me

   The Martian's ship is a dirty mess from traveling through our atmosphere and the crew is anxious to get it washed but it won't fit through the BP car wash next door. Draw a map instructing the Martians to the Plaza car wash. The Martians do not understand our written words, or north, east, south, or west, or right or left but they do recognize numbers. Add landmarks that the aliens will be able to recognize when they see them from the air. Then proceed toward the Children's Room and look under the stairway. Take your map with you.

6. *Color-coded envelopes with instructions and one roll of toilet paper for each team are waiting under the stairway. Markers, tape, and children's books about Ohio are on the table nearby.*

   Good Hosts

   Our visitors have come a long way and we should give them a gift to take home to remember us by. An Ambassador Quilt is a perfect gift but it is very warm on Mars. Fortunately, our toilet tissue has the same consistency as a very fine cool fabric on Mars. A tastefully woven wall hanging with an outline map of Ohio, our state flag, our state bird, and state flower, signed by all your team members would be a thoughtful gift. You may take your fine fabric to the table by the display case to work on your gift. Once completed, proceed to the round tables in the children's room. Take your quilt with you.

7. *Color-coded envelopes with instructions for each team are waiting at the tables with paper plates, play dough, and a few play dough tools: plastic knives and rolling pins.*

Soup's On

Food on Earth is so varied, the Martians are confused about what we eat. Make a model of a typical American meal to show them what we like to eat. Display it attractively on the plate provided. Then check the Internet terminal at the reference desk. Take your meal with you.

8. *Color-coded envelopes with instructions for each team are waiting at the reference desk with a Web site address for the lyrics for Weird Al's Star Wars song.*

Tune In

Music is important on Mars and our visitors want to expand their musical knowledge. The lyrics to one of their favorite pieces is located here: www.sagabegins.com/lyrics.html. Print off a copy of the lyrics and go to the small meeting room in the back of the children's room. *Color-coded envelopes with instructions for each team are waiting with a tape recorder, blank tape and a helper—play this tape later during the lock-in! Very funny!*

Your team may record a verse or two of this song (sung to the tune of "American Pie"). Start recording where the tape is stopped, and stop the tape when finished. Do not rewind! And now it is time to look at the geochron clock on the wall by the display case.

9. *Color-coded envelopes with instructions for each team are waiting by the clock.*

Just Watch Me

The Martians have to leave when the sun comes up here. Take a look at the geochron clock to see how many hours till sunup in our part of the world. To remind them when it is time to leave, we will need to give them watches! Each team member construct a watch with the materials provided and wear them. The materials are on the table by the copier. When finished, put on your watch and take a look out the south windows of the library.

The easiest instructions to make for this is to make a watch for a sample. This is the messiest, yet a fun part of the hunt. Provide a box of Rainbow Vanilla wafers for the watch faces, frosting in tubes to draw the hands or numbers of the watch face, yarn for tying, and snack sized baggies with holes punched in each end for the yarn ties. To assemble, choose a cookie, draw on the hands with frosting, slip into baggie, zip shut, attach yarn ties to each end and tie on wrist for wearing. The team members will have to help each other tie them on. You will need extra cookies and frosting for nibbling.

10. *Color-coded envelopes with instructions for each team are waiting on the south windowsill with pencils and paper. The gas station sign can be seen from the window. Calculators are waiting at the reference desk.*

Aliens Go Home

What is the price per gallon of premium gasoline tonight?

Find the distance from Earth to Mars tonight on the reference computer at this site: http://space.jpl.nasa.gov/

1 kilometer = .6 miles

The Martian spaceship gets 100,000 mpg

How much gasoline will they need to get back home?

How much will it cost if they buy premium gas at the BP station next door?

When you have THAT figured out, bring all your findings back to the headquarters (large meeting room). Your collections will be judged! You will earn one-five points for each task accomplished!

In the meeting room, have a row of tables along the wall divided so each team can display their findings. While the teens eat, you and any adult helpers you may have judge each of the ten findings by awarding points for attempting the activity, following instructions, accuracy, creativity, and presentation (one point for each for 50 total possible points). When points are totaled, announce teams, highest points to lowest. As a team is announced, they go to the prize table to choose a prize. Everyone gets a prize, but high scorers get first choice.

Figure 8–1 We Have a Mission Team.
A more serious team of researchers could not be found?

Figure 8–2 We Have a Mission Team.
The green team listens to their recording of "A Legend Begins."

Library Survivor

Like the space theme scavenger hunt, the teens must use their library skills to get to the fun in Library Survivor! The Summer Reading Program theme for the 2001 summer was travel and a very popular program on TV was Survivor. This hunt was the opening activity for a Beach Party Lock-In.

Print the instructions on different colors of paper for each team and cut apart for distributing to the different stations. Teams may be selected by drawing slips of colored paper or just form the teams as the teens arrive. The notes in italics are descriptions of what needs to be prepared and in place ahead of time. Distribute a sheet of paper with the following paragraph followed by a numbered list, one-ten, to each player with a pencil. Each team will need a bag for collecting.

> The object of this game is to use your library skills to find the materials you need to collect to survive. First discover where you need to go, then do whatever is required when you get there! You will be rewarded with fish for your accomplishments! Fish earned throughout this evening may be used to buy prizes at the fish auction at the end of the lock-in. Your first task is posted at the computer catalogs by the main entrance. Take only the materials marked for your team. When using the computer catalogs, remember you can limit your searches to Coshocton's holdings. (There are no interlibrary loans on deserted islands!) You can always ask a librarian for help . . . for a price.

Place instructions in envelopes marked with team colors (mark all envelopes with team colors and task numbers so there is no confusion) at the computer catalog stations.

1. Use the catalog to locate books that would help you identify the trees and find them on the shelves. Write the call number on your sheet by # 1. Hint: subject search, trees identification.
    Place in envelopes in the tree book section along with green paper, tape, yarn, and a hole puncher.
    Task #1 Leaf me alone!
    Leaves can be very useful for survival! Make a hat to protect yourself from the sun! Use the materials you find here. Extra fish awarded for high fashion leaf hats! When you are finished, head for the reference desk . . . The LIBRARIAN has some questions for you!
2. *A reference librarian is sitting at the desk and cards with questions are face down on the desk. He also has a box of pencils (logs) and a ball of string (rope). The teens will choose a question card for the librarian to ask and the team must answer correctly to earn a log or piece of rope. The questions were about our library and staff. A sampler of the questions:*

Are fiction books shelved by the author's first name, last name, or the state they were born in?

True or false: Nonfiction books are filed by the Dewey system because they are all wet.

If you lose your library card, how much does it cost to get a new one?

Name one thing you can do on the Internet besides chat.

True or false: If you return a book late, it goes on your permanent record.

Can you name three reference librarians?

True or false: The poetry board decides what poetry books to buy.

What is the fine per day for overdue YA books?

A Task #2 envelope for each team has the following message:
Task #2 When is the next raft out of here?
Your team can work together to answer the librarian's questions. For each correct answer, he will give you a "log" or some "rope." When you have collected enough, you need to build a raft if you ever want to leave here! Ask the librarian to write the number of questions your team answered correctly by # 2. When you are finished, go to the computer catalog in the YA room.

3. *Instructions in #3 envelopes at YA catalog:*
Accidents seem to happen when you are marooned, so FIRST AID is important to know! Use the catalog to locate first-aid books and go to that shelf. Write the call number by # 3. Hint: subject search, first aid in illness and injury.
Bandage and sling materials for each team are placed in a basket by the first-aid books.
Task #3 Oh my aching head. . . .
Oh my, your team is accident prone! One member has a head injury, one hurt his ankle, one a wrist, and the last one needs his arm in a sling! Give each other the necessary first aid with the materials provided for your team and then proceed to the tables in the adult magazine area.

4. *Instructions for each team in #4 envelopes in the Magazine area and markers, paper, and rulers:*
Task #4 Where in the world are we? Draw a map of the main floor of the library. Designate the following items essential for your survival in the library on your map.

1. YA room   2. Reference desk   3. Main desk

4. Pay phone   5. Copy machine   6. Internet computers
7. Computer catalogs   8. Video room   9. Restroom
10. Water fountain

Use the materials available on the tables to make your maps. When you are finished, go to the computer catalogs by the main entrance again and find the envelope #5 for your team.

5. *Instructions in #5 envelopes at catalogs:*
    Fish are the one thing you need to find tonight to get those great prizes at the auction! Use the catalog to find a Q book on fishing (that's your hint). Find a fishing book in the Q section and go to that shelf! Write the call number by #5 on your collection sheet.
    The instructions at the Q fishing books will say to go to the fishing station. Prepare the station by marking off lines on the floor with masking tape. The distance is determined by how much ceiling room you have for flipping! Scuba flippers, sea critter beanie babies, and a fish net are all you need (all borrowed or on hand). One teen flips while the rest of his team try to catch the beanies in the net.
    Task #5 Gone fishing
    There is more than one way to catch a fish . . . and many other water creatures! Elect one team member to be the flipper and the others hold the net. The object is to flip those critters into the net before they skitter away. Rules are, you stay behind the lines and only one flip per critter! You may take turns flipping. Record how many critters your team catches! Write the number of sea critters your team catches by #5. When you are finished, proceed to the computer catalogs in the children's room.

6. *On the shelf beside the book Treasure Island, place envelopes for each team with a hint where to find their team's treasure—hidden in a different place for each team. The treasure is a baggie of gold foil covered chocolate coins with a big X on top, color coordinated to each team. The fish monger, unknown to the players at this point, will award according to how much of the treasure makes it to the end of the hunt!*
    Treasure hints are:

    > *Your treasure is where you sign up for the Internet in the children's room.*
    > *Your treasure is under a comfy place to sit and read near here.*
    > *Your treasure is where you can find a book for your baby sister or brother.*
    > *Your treasure is where you can find a Disney video.*
    > *Your treasure is above the J biographies.*
    > *Your treasure is in the small meeting room.*

At the catalogs, envelopes for Task 6:

Task #6 X marks the spot!

Who wrote the classic novel *Treasure Island?* Write the author's last name at #6. Hint: title search. Find the book on the shelf in the children's room and pick up your team's envelope to discover where your treasure is! When you find it, head back to the children's room catalog! Look for your team's #7.

7. *Instructions in envelopes for Task # 7:*

Use the catalog to locate books that would help you identify the BUGS in the adult section. Write the call number by #7. Hint: subject search, insects identification.

Materials for basket weaving—paper or raffia will do, scissors, and gummy bugs and worms are placed near the bug identification books. The gummy critters are on separate plates for each team. The fish monger will award according to the number of critters that make it to the end of the hunt!

Task #7 I'm not eating that!

Well, maybe later when you get really hungry these will look more appetizing! You need to weave a little basket to carry them in with the materials provided for your team. When you have collected the bugs and critters, it is time to go to the YA room catalog again and look for your team's Task #8.

8. *Instructions in envelope for task #8 placed by catalog:*

Supposedly you can figure out where you are by looking at the stars. Find where there are YA books about constellations (that's your hint). Write the call number by #8.

Make some canned constellations . . . cans with the ends punched in a constellation design, or any kind of tube with the end covered with black paper with the constellation design punched into it. I made mine with six pop cans. I covered the outside with blue paper, drew the constellation picture on the outside with silver dots for the stars, and punched holes in the bottom of the can with a nail. Number each can. They could look at the picture on the side and also see what the constellation would look like in the sky by looking in the can. Note that when punching holes, you need to make the constellation design in reverse on the bottom for it to appear correctly! Place the cans on the shelf by the constellation and space books.

Task #8 Twinkle Twinkle

Identify the canned constellations! Write the names of the constellations you see in the cans by holding them up to a light on the paper provided for your team. Make sure your answers match the numbers on the cans. When you are finished, we still need to work on food gathering, so back to the catalog to see if we can identify the birds here.

9. *Envelopes for Task #9 at the catalog:*
   Find where bird books are. Hint: subject keyword, birds identification.
   Write the call number by # 9.
   Gotta love those beanie babies. A badminton racket, bird beanies, and a fish landing net make a great bird catching game! Once again, tape lines on the floor fitting the room you have for batting those birds. We positioned the batter up on the mezzanine and the catcher with the net below on the main floor.
   Task #9 Bye Bye Birdie
   Lucky for us there are lots of birds here if you can catch them. Use the bird catching equipment provided to see how many you can catch. Elect one team member to bat birds and one to catch them in the net. All team members take a turn. BUT you only get one chance at each bird before it flies away! Record how many birds your team catches. I think we better signal for some help here . . . Go to the YA room!

10. *Envelopes for Task #10 on the counter with sea shell macaroni, sandpaper or brown paper, and Tacky glue:*
    Task #10 HELP!
    You will find the materials you need to write a help message in the YA room. BUT your rescuers only know SPANISH! Use what you have learned to find a Spanish/English dictionary to find out what you need to write! When you have all of your tasks finished, take them to the fish monger (your YA librarian) to collect your fish. (If you need a hint who the YA librarian is, it will cost you LOTS of fish!)

When a team finishes the hunt, they bring the record sheet and their collection with them to the fish monger (the YA librarian) who awards fish for each activity based on: attempting the activity, following instructions, accuracy, creativity, and how many gummy creatures and how much treasure made it to the end. The fish were colorful clip art fish printed on card stock, cut apart, and "netted" in a potato sack. Any misbehavior that didn't subside with a warning cost players some of their winnings! The fish were used for the fish auction at the end of the evening to buy prizes. The more fish they won by doing the hunt well, the more prizes they could afford.

Note: No beanie babies were injured in the performance of this scavenger hunt!

Figure 8–3 Library Survivor Program.
A team tries to earn materials to build a raft by answering the librarian's questions.

Figure 8–4 Library Survivor Program.
As their teammates go fishing for sea critters, these two try to save the catch of the day.

Library Tour

This is a simple fast scavenger hunt to use when giving tours to teens. Build a hunt by writing down all the rooms you will visit in the order of the tour, and then write a question for each of those rooms. Type it up, make copies, and pass them out to your teens with pencils then take them on the tour. They will help each other, which makes it a social activity and the hunt encourages them to be more observant during the tour. When conducting the tour, tell about the room first and then give them a few minutes to find the answer to their question. Small prizes can be awarded for the most correct answers or everyone can win a library pencil or magnet.

A sample Library Tour hunt follows:

1. Meeting Room: Where is the first-aid kit for the Meeting Room?
2. Book Store: How much do videos cost in the bookstore?
3. Magazine Stacks: How many years of Time Magazine does the library own?
4. Preservation Department: Where is the bindery?
5. Basement Storage: How many shades of pink paper does the library have?
6. Local History: What did N. 9th St used to be called?
7. Young Adult: What events are happening for teens this month?
8. Fiction Collection: What science fiction authors on Coshocton's shelves begin with the letter Z?
9. Children's Room: What kinds of books are featured in the special display area today?
10. Main Desk: What is the URL for the Coshocton Public Library's homepage?
11. Video Room: How much are video fines per day?
12. Newspapers and Periodicals: Which newspaper is "No. 1 in the USA"?
13. Mezzanine: How old was William Green when he died?
14. Office: How many people are on vacation in June?
15. Reference: Who and when does one say "gardyloo"?
16. Internet Terminals: What does OPLIN stand for?

Independent Scavenger Hunts

Scavenger hunts can be played as independent programs. Print copies of the lists of questions and hints. Teens can pick up the scavenger hunt questions during a study hall in a school library or when they visit the public library, and finish it during their visit. The finished hunts can be turned in at a drawing box and a winner drawn from all correct entries. An alternative is that the hunt can be graded by a librarian as it is turned in. A small prize can be awarded to each teen for completion. To create a hunt, choose what you want the teens to learn, then write questions that will lead them to discover a new fact or resource at the library.

THE BOTTOM LINE

Scavenger hunts are free programs if you use what you have on hand or what you can borrow. Prizes are where your expense will be and awarding them can be part of the fun too. It is great if you can get prizes that go with the theme. For the Space Mission, I had a table of Star Wars t-shirts and posters that I had received from Naeir. The teams went up to choose their prizes according to how many points they earned from the judging—the teams with the highest points getting first choice.

For Library Survivor, I held a fish auction at the end of the evening for the prizes. The teens could buy prizes according to how many fish they had earned during the hunt. The prizes were summer clearance items (inflatable coolers, floats, hats, sports bottles, shell ankle bracelets) I was able to get at a great discount from Gadzooks, a mall store teens love.

If you are doing the Library Tour or passive scavenger hunt, library pencils, candy, book marks, newsletters, coupons for $1.00 off fines, or a free replacement card in a book bag is a perfect reward for finishing the hunt. Sandy Marvin, Coshocton High School librarian, uses the copier money to buy prizes for her students and reports good success using scavenger hunts to encourage improvement of library skills.

THE COLLECTION CONNECTION

Include any part of the collection or area of the library that you want the teens to explore in your hunt. I choose subjects that fit the theme and several that students often request for assignments for the lock-in hunts. I think any student that found gummy worms and bugs on a shelf will remember where to find the right book when he has to do a bug collection!

RESOURCES

Education World [Online]. *Scavenger Hunts: Searching for Treasure on the Internet!* Available: www.education-world.com/a_curr/curr113.shtml [2002, May 14].

Library Scavenger Hunt [Online]. Available: www.mowyn.com/scavenger/online.htm [2002, May 16].

McCutcheon, Randall, and Pamela Espeland. 1991. *Can You Find It?: 25 Library Scavenger Hunts to Sharpen Your Research Skills, rev. ed.* Minneapolis: Free Spirit Publishing.

Chapter 9

Lock-Ins and Holiday Parties

OVERVIEW

The difference between teen parties and lock-ins is the length of time you need to provide food, entertainment, and supervision. Lock-ins are held after the library closes and can be for a few hours or all night, depending on your stamina and available helpers. Our lock-in programs are held in August on a Friday night from 8 p.m. to midnight. If your town has a curfew, contact the sheriff department to let them know you will be releasing teens at midnight or that there will be teens in the building all night.

A BASIC LOCK-IN PLAN

The teens can pre-register for the lock-in and upon arrival sign in and give an emergency phone number. This can be used in case of accident or illness but also in case of any severe behavioral problems that can't be controlled. You may also request a permission slip signed by a parent. Grades 7–12 are invited and attendance is limited to about 20 teens at our lock-ins.

A good opening event is a group activity that allows the teens to explore the library. It is exciting for the teens to be in the library when all the lighting isn't on and no one else is there. Schedule extra adult help for this first part of the program. Your helpers can leave after the opening activity when group is contained in a smaller area for the rest of the lock-in. For the opening activity, a scavenger hunt (see Chapter 8) or a version of the Live Clue (see Chapter 6) game works well. Our lock-ins follow the summer reading program and all of these activities can be adapted to the summer's reading theme or the Teen Read Week theme.

After roaming the library during these activities, we all move to the meeting room for the rest of the lock-in where food is an important next event. The food can be a fun part of the program by having a pizza taste-off or the teens can make the food themselves with tacos in a bag, a salad or potato bar, and a sundae bar or fondue for dessert. The rest of the evening can be a variety of games, crafts, and activities, where the teens can move from one activity to another, forming smaller groups. Internet time, dancing, talent shows, and games are all possible activities to add. A closing group activity is nice to wind things up and can be an event that will reward prizes or party favors to take home. At our last lock-in, we had an auction. The teens bought their prizes with the fish they had earned during the Library Survivor scavenger hunt. A periodic door prize drawing is fun, too. When planning an overnight, keep in mind a number of chaperones will be needed, schedule quiet activities to lead up to times for reading and sleeping, plan acceptable sleeping arrangements for boys and girls, and set rules about where the teens are supposed to be and what is acceptable behavior. Know what you are going to do if anyone intentionally breaks your rules. Explain before an incident that parents will be called no matter what time it is! For an all-nighter, serve a light breakfast before pick-up time.

Medieval Theme

To close the Medieval Summer Reading Program, the lock-in began with Castle Clue, a medieval version of Live Clue. "Monty Python and the Holy Grail" played on video (which many of the teens have memorized) while we ate pizza and the rest of the evening was spent playing board games and a hide and seek game called "Sardines" and a noisy card game called "Spoons." The rules for Spoons can be found at www.pagat.com/eights/spoons.html and Sardines is explained in the More Party and Lock-In Activities section of this chapter.

Space Theme

The space themed Summer Reading Program inspired the "We Have a Mission" scavenger hunt. The Live Clue game could also be adapted to this theme with each room being a different planet or science fiction world: the Star Trek Room, the Star Wars Room, the Martian Chronicles Room, etc. Characters from these stories could be the suspects and weapons could be phasers, lasers, disrupters, photon torpedoes, Vulcan death grip (!). UFO pizzas made with biscuit dough and a variety of toppings could provide an activity and food for the lock-in. Decorating cookies or Jiffy cakes with a space theme (alien faces, landscapes, space ships) would be a fun creative activity. The teens could vote for the winning design and dessert is ready. Any science fiction video or theme music would provide atmosphere. Paint t-shirts with favorite science fiction designs for a craft activity.

Beach Party Theme

A scavenger hunt, Library Survivor, was the opening activity for the Beach Party Lock-In. Our summer reading theme had been geography and travel and a very popular show on television that summer, Survivor, was set on an island. We set up our own island beach party right in our meeting room. First, all tables and chairs were removed. The walls were decorated with fish wrapping paper below chair rail height for ocean water and everything above was treated as sky. Blue crepe paper streamers or ribbon can be used to create ocean waves on the walls. A variety of sea life bulletin board cut-outs borrowed from the children's department and a large yellow sun with sunglasses made from paper helped decorate the walls. The window to the kitchen was decorated to look like a bamboo hut with a thatched roof using brown kraft paper. A thatched look can be created by fringing the paper with a paper cutter and layering the fringed pieces, taping them to the wall. Palm trees in the corners were constructed of wrapping paper and poster board. Furniture was limited to beach chairs, beach towels, and floats. A large, shiny, blue tarp was placed on the floor for a "pool." Travel posters on the walls with tropical destinations added to the beach atmosphere. A volleyball net tied to two chairs was set up at one end of the room. A fan with ribbons tied on the grid provided an ocean breeze. A baby pool full of "seaweed" and small prizes and a treasure chest of big prizes sat in the corners.

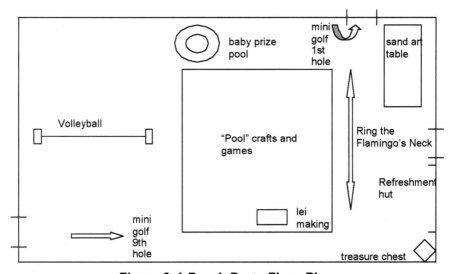

Figure 9–1 Beach Party Floor Plan.
A meeting room can be the scene for a Beach Party. Designate areas for action games, sitting games, crafts, and food.

Figure 9–2 Beach Party Room.
This Beach Party room is ready to jump into for a sunny good time.

GAMES, CRAFTS, AND ACTIVITIES FOR A BEACH PARTY

- Lei Making: Pull silk flowers off old candle rings and artificial bouquets. (Collect from staff, family, and friends.) The teens string them together using fishing line or dental floss with a needle. Tie off at the desired length. The greenery left over can go into the baby pool for seaweed to hide the small prizes.
- Sand Art: Make in baby food jars as explained in the crafts chapter. Spray paint the lids and hot glue a small shell on top ahead of time and let the teens choose a container and lid and be creative with the colored sand.
- Beach Blanket Bingo: Create bingo cards with the word BEACH across the top using a bingo card-generating program or make your own cards. A bingo software program will print the cards with the words in different positions and also print out the calling cards. Beach words, rather than numbers were used on the cards. Use small seashells or wrapped candy for markers.
- Beach Ball Volleyball: Volleyball inside the meeting room? Well, this version anyway! Players sit on their beach towels and use a beach ball. Keep the net low for ceiling clearance by tying it to two chairs.

B	E	A	C	H
Bikini	Sand	Jet ski	Seafood	Pail
Basket	Boogie board	Tattoos	Clam	Towel
Burn	Surf	FREE SPACE	Minigolf	Shore
Blanket	Sun	Sailboats	Reading	Sunscreen
Umbrella	Sand castles	Tan	Marina	Raft

Figure 9–3 Beach Blanket Bingo Card.
Bingo cards can be created with a beach party theme.

- Sea Shell Mancala: Mancala is an ancient game you can play with any-thing from stones to jelly beans. For the beach party, clam shells were used for the playing pieces, small paper plates were used for the cups and a sand bucket was placed on each end for the mancalas.
- Grass Skirt Hula Contest: Hawaiian music, grass skirts, and leis . . . just a lovely thought unless you put them on the guys and the girls are the judges!
- Hula Hoop Contest: Just like it sounds, who can hula hoop the long-est? Who has the best moves?
- Coconut Bowling: Place a bowling pin in the center of a hula hoop on the floor. Using coconuts for bowling balls, trying to roll the coconut into the hoop without knocking over the pin.
- Mini Putt Putt: Use toddler sized golf sets and set up a course through a few rooms or set up obstacles in the meeting room. Provide score cards.
- Ring the Flamingo's Neck: Play this game like horseshoes. You need two lawn flamingos and rings cut from heavy cardboard. Anchor the flamingos in two foot long 2 x 6's by drilling holes for the wire legs or by sticking the wire legs in buckets of sand. Decorate with some greenery

and leis. Place tape on the floor to mark where players must stand to toss the rings.

FOOD FOR A BEACH PARTY

Hotdogs, fruit kabobs and Goldfish crackers or chips, sodas or fruit punch, ice cream or Popsicles—summer food fits the beach theme. Serve from the thatched hut.

PRIZES FOR A BEACH PARTY

Prizes for games can be sunglasses, sunscreen, water guns, candy, beach balls; there are lots of inexpensive fun items teens would like that would add to the beach atmosphere. Throughout the evening the teens were permitted to cash in fish (tickets with fish pictures on them) to search the baby pool for small prizes hidden in the seaweed or they could choose to save the fish for the auction at the end of the evening for the larger prizes displayed in the treasure chest. Small prizes included lip balm, comics, posters, badges, nail polish, collector cards, and any other small items we had on hand.

The treasure chest was a box wrapped in gold paper with a sign on the front that said "treasure chest." The treasure chest prizes were auctioned off during the last half hour of the night and the teens loved this! They were busily counting their fish and figuring what they wanted to bid on and how high they could go. Everyone went home with neat prizes they had earned by using their library skills during the Library Survivor game. Some of the prizes in our treasure chest were inflatable coolers, floats, Caboodle kits, water bottles, and Frisbees.

MORE PARTY AND LOCK-IN ACTIVITIES

Pizza Taste-Off

A Pizza Taste-Off was combined with a game show for a Teen Read Week program. Our local pizza parlors were happy to participate and the teens had a great time judging the pizza and eating it too!

Call the area pizza establishments and ask if they would like to participate in a pizza taste-off to help celebrate Teen Read Week or other event at the library. I asked for a donation of two large uncut cheese pizzas. Some businesses offered to deliver, which was very helpful, and some we had to pick up.

Two long tables were reserved for the pizzas with numbered place cards for the trays of pizza. Each teen received a large divided Styrofoam plate with the sections numbered along the edges with a permanent marker. Large trays were also numbered and so were the pizza boxes so we wouldn't get mixed up about which pizza goes where and which ones they were tasting.

The pizzas were smuggled into the library out of sight of the teens. We cut all the pizza into strips (scissors work pretty well for this!), placed them on the coordinating numbered trays and placed the trays on the tables by the coordinating numbered cards. For example, the Domino's Pizza box would have a number one, the tray we put the pieces of Domino's pizza on would have a number one and the tray would be placed by the number one card on the pizza tasting table. Each teen took one strip of pizza from each tray for the judging, placing the pieces in the sections of the tray matching the place card numbers.

The teens voted on a ballot by the number of the pizza and after turning the ballot in, they could help themselves to more of their favorites. The teens were sure they could identify their own favorites just by sight, but with seven different cheese pizzas, it was trickier than they thought. The ballot asked them to judge for best crust, best sauce, and best cheese individually, and then best overall pizza. During the intermission of the game show, the winners for each category were announced. Thank-you notes were sent to all the pizza establishments for their donations and I told them if they won in a category.

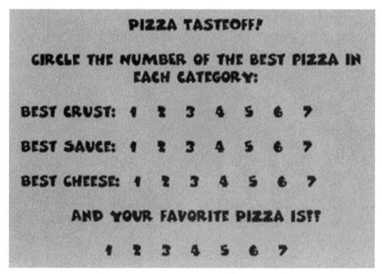

Figure 9–4 Pizza Taste-Off Ballot.
Teens voted for their favorite pizza on a ballot. The votes were tallied and winners announced during the game show intermission.

Fun Party Food Ideas

Teens like to play with their food! The following ideas provide an activity and a treat for parties and lock-ins.

Chocolate fondue: Melt 1 cup semi-sweet chocolate chips, stir in 1 cup whipping cream. Keep warm in fondue pot or mini crock pot. Dip fruit pieces, marshmallows, or angel food cake squares into the chocolate with wooden skewers. (Remind teens not to eat off the skewers; provide forks for eating the fondue from their plates.)

Make your own sundae bar: Dip ice cream into bowls, let the teens build their own sundaes with a variety of toppings available in bowls with spoons.

Assemble your own pizza: Use canned biscuit dough or crescent roll dough. Teens design the shape of the crust, add their own toppings. Bake and serve. The sauce is easier to manage if you put it in plastic squeeze bottles. The teens should wear plastic gloves if adding toppings from bowls by hand. An alternative is an adult (wearing gloves or using tongs) serving out an amount of each topping to each teen from a large bowl on to a plate.

Make a hero: Provide hero buns, cold cuts, cheese, and sandwich toppings. Teens make their own hero. Once again, use gloves and/or utensils when handling food from the group supply.

Tacos in a bag: Gently crush a snack sized bag of Doritos. Add a spoon of taco filling (keep warm in a crock pot). Teens add taco toppings: lettuce, taco sauce, cheese, sour cream, onions. Serve with a fork.

Slice and bake cookies: Easy and fast but smells so good! Teens slice and bake and decorate cookies. The rolls of cookies are available with holiday designs for holiday parties and TAB meetings.

Rice Krispie treats: 2 cups miniature marshmallows, 1-1/2 tablespoons of butter, and 6 cups of Rice Krispies. Melt butter and marshmallows in microwave two-three minutes, stirring once or twice. Add Rice Krispies, spread in pan, and cool. Variations: add 1/4 cup peanut butter to marshmallow; add raisins and peanuts; add cinnamon red hot candies.

Scavenger snack mix: Each teen has a scavenger hunt question in the library. When he finds the answer, an ingredient for the snack mix is waiting for him there. Teens return to the meeting room and contribute their findings to a large bowl. Mix and serve. Ingredient suggestions: nuts, raisins, candy corn, Chex cereal, pretzel sticks, cheese crackers, Cheerios, M&Ms.

Christmas Carry-In Dinner

Our December TAB meeting is a carry-in dinner. I provide a meat dish of some kind (ham, Kentucky Fried Chicken) and the teens all sign up at the November meeting to bring everything else. After eating dinner, we play games and visit and I give each teen a gift bag with small holiday items that

I have collected from Naeir, such as an ornament, stickers, gift tags, cosmetics, collector cards, pencils, lip balm, etc. Games we have played include Pictionary®, Christmas Carol word scrambles, and the following anthropology game I made up that turned out to be very fun and funny. The story may be adapted to your community's landmarks. Imagine what changes might take place geographically and culturally in 20,000 years!

ANTHROPOLOGY GAME: IN THE YEAR 20001

The teens are to imagine they are anthropologists in the year 20001. Each table or group is given a copy of the following passage and a Wal-Mart (choose your own local department store) bag of items. Included in each bag are some odd Christmas decorations, toys, office equipment, etc. The object is for the teens to be creative in developing theories about the uses of the items in the year 2000 (current year) and to have fun doing so. After the teams have about 15 minutes or so to look over their bag of artifacts and develop and take notes about their theories, announce that they must choose a spokesperson for their team to present their theories to the whole group. Each team spokesperson then presents their theories using their artifacts as props to illustrate. Our TAB board had a lot of laughs and so did we adults with this activity! One of my favorite conclusions came from a group that had a small stuffed Santa in a cellophane wrapper (a cryogenically preserved ancient human in the traditional tribal clothing from the time period). His home was a Santa hat propped up like a tipi and a jar candle that just happened to be the perfect size was a chair that doubled as a "waste receptacle."

The handout for the teams has the following journal entry and an area at the bottom of the page for a team member to record ideas. Read the passage aloud:

Journal Entry for December 18, 20001:
The NO-L group, our team of anthropologists, made a startling discovery today along the banks of the Muskingum Sea, where recent storms have washed away the beach area to reveal a massive expanse that appears to have been a center for the Christmas celebration, held in the "winter season" (a cold period of the year before The Great Earthquake). Today in our excavation, we have uncovered something that may help us piece together the symbolism and tradition that was Christmas. We have known from the famous Hallmark site excavated in 19982 that Christmas was a birthday celebration of Saint Nicholas who was called Jesus as a child. It is believed that he celebrated his own birthday by giving valuable gifts to well-behaved children while giving bad children foot coverings and undergarments that were not to be seen by anyone so it would appear they received no gifts at all. He recorded

children's names on lists thought to go in their permanent records and future employers would look at these and determine the person's wage and societal status. We have not yet determined the purpose for many of the artifacts discovered in today's excavation but they are believed to be a sack of the valuable gifts! The sack itself is blue in color, the sides and bottom appear to have been sealed by melting. Two holes along the open edge are thought to be for hooking over the steering mechanism of two-wheeled transport vehicles used at the time. There appears to be a word on the side of the sack, "Wal-Mart." It is curious that the inhabitants of the area would misspell the name of such an important site. We have seen evidence of the four walls. Some items in the bag were wrapped in large pieces of glossy paper derived from cellulose fibers decorated with symbols. The paper was held in place by unidirectional bonding strips and bound by brightly colored bands. Other items were wrapped in clear cellophane—one wonders if it was a safety or preservation measure. It had been earlier concluded that the Christmas holiday was only a one-day celebration, but the date on a small piece of paper found in the bag was November 24, 2000. We now believe Christmas was held over a longer period leading us to believe there were many more children than there are now. The details of the excavated items and their uses as determined by our team of highly professional and intelligent anthropologists are:
(Leave room for note taking at the end of the passage.)

Halloween Decorating Party

Our October TAB meeting is a work party. Our task is to decorate the meeting room for the children's Halloween parties later in the week. They have a lot of fun doing that project alone, but a few treats and a game or two makes it a party for the teens, too. The children's department provides a big box of all kinds of decorations (from Naeir!). The teens sometimes make a plan and sometimes decorate haphazardly, but they have fun and the children like the results. Rice Krispie treats or slice and bake cookies with Halloween shapes in them, and microwave popcorn make good snacks for some of the teens to make during the decorating party.

THE MUMMY WRAP

The teens are paired off and each couple is given a roll of toilet tissue. The couple must decide who will be the mummy and who will be the wrapper. When given the GO signal, they begin wrapping. Prizes are given to the couple who used their entire roll first and to the team who made the best mummy.

Figure 9–5 The Mummy Wrap.
All wrapped up and no place to go? The Mummy Wrap is a fun activity as a reward for a work meeting.

Human Bingo

At a party, lock-in, or a TAB meeting a Human Bingo game is a fun ice breaker. Sheets of paper, with a 5 x 5 grid of squares large enough to write a few words, and pencils are all you need. Write common and some not so common teen activities, one in each square. The order doesn't matter and you can make one card and photocopy to save time. The squares do not need to be mixed up as in regular bingo games. The teens' task is to find others in the room who have done the activities and have those people sign those squares. They may sign their own cards only once. The first teen to collect five signatures in a row is the winner. They must get up and move around and talk to each other to play this game. Often what you hear is something similar to "I play in the band, what do you do?" They will overhear each other so the game moves rather quickly. Each person may sign each card only once. After there is a first winner, the game can be continued for another round. The first person to get signatures for all the squares wins this second round. Depending upon the number of teens playing, they may need to sign the cards more than once to cover all the squares in the second round.

I like to read comics	My favorite author is David Eddings	I'm a Cleveland Indians fan	I play the trumpet	I'm graduating high school this year
My dad's a dentist	I like to draw	I know karate	My mom is a page at the library	I love the science fair
I ride horses	I play tennis	FREE SPACE	I play soccer	I'm a Harry Potter Fan
I play the flute	I play the piano	I like mysteries	I play percussion	I like to sing
I write poetry	I am a Star Wars fan	I am a J.R.R. Tolkien fan	I like romance novels	I have a job

Figure 9–6 Human Bingo Card.
A Human Bingo game is a great ice breaker. Customize the cards to your teens talents and interests.

VARIATIONS

Try titles of YA books or movies in the squares. If the teens have read the book or seen the movie, they sign the square. When making this game for my TAB, I looked on their applications to find out what their extra-curricular activities were and used several of those. Leave some time for discussion. The teens may have found others with shared interests, or they may want to talk about their activities, books, or movies.

Mad Libs

Write out a familiar passage from a book, a poem, or song lyrics on a flipchart, leaving numbered blanks for names, nouns, verbs, adjectives, and adverbs. With the writing facing away from the group, you or a teen volunteer writes the teens' suggestions in the blanks. To play the game, ask the teens to suggest names, nouns, verbs, adjectives, and adverbs for each number as needed. For example, if the first blank needs a name, ask someone for a name. As answers are suggested, write them in the blanks. When all the blanks are filled, read the new version to the group. A passage from a romance book would work for a Valentine's party, a horror book for a Halloween party, a Christmas carol for a Christmas party, or a familiar poem for Poetry Night.

Dictionary

This game is fun in a group. You can use cards from a Balderdash game, make your own word cards, or use special jargon or lingo dictionaries. Each player needs small slips of paper and a pencil. One player chooses a word from the cards or dictionaries that he thinks will be unfamiliar to the group. The players all write down the word and what they think the word means, creating a definition if they have no idea. The player who chooses the word also writes the word and the correct definition on a slip. All of the slips are passed to this player, who reads them to the group in random order. Each player must vote for the definition he thinks is correct. Points are earned when a player guesses a correct definition and when any player's definition gets a vote, even if it is incorrect. That player has "balderdashed" another. After points are tallied for that round, the next player gets to choose the next word.

Sardines

Sardines is a variation of hide and seek. The basement of the library was the perfect setting for this game. The teens are all packed like sardines in one space to start the game. They seem to think the smaller the space, the better. One leaves and hides. After a few minutes the rest of the teens start seeking for him. If anyone finds him, he hides with him too. This continues until everyone is packed in the new hiding spot like sardines. Then the game starts over when the last person who found them leaves to hide. This game continues until they tire of it!

Sweet Heart Chat

Candy conversation hearts are passed around to all the teens. The object of the game is to create a conversation between two players using the candy hearts they have. Prize for the longest conversation that makes any sense is a box of conversation hearts!

Twenty Questions

A player chooses a familiar book title or character. Other players may ask up to 20 questions that can be answered by a yes or no answer to try to determine the title or character.

Play-Doh Sculptionary

Junior Pictionary® has game cards to use for this game. Instead of drawing clues on paper, Play-Doh® is used to sculpt a figure for the team to guess the answer, and no words are allowed from the sculptor. Follow the same rules as the traditional Pictionary® game.

Name That Tune

An electronic keyboard, a book of Christmas carol music or children's tunes, and some trivia about each song is all you need for this game. Two teams send up one player at a time. A bit of trivia is read by the MC and the players start off bidding to answer the name of the song in the least number of notes played on the keyboard. A player can say "I can name that tune in four notes." The other player may say "I can name that tune in three notes!" When one teen stops bidding, he says "Name that tune!" The bid number of notes is played, and the other player must name that tune. If he is correct, his team earns a point and the play moves on to two more teens. If the answer is incorrect, his opponent can hear the number of notes he asked for in his last bid. This game can be played with popular music, too, offering trivia about the performers.

THE BOTTOM LINE

Lock-ins and holiday parties are going to cost a bit more than shorter programs because you are providing more food with a combination of other activities. I try to make use of materials I have on hand, and borrow as much I can and save the money for the food and prizes. I was able to acquire an incredible box of cool summer prizes for $50.00 from an end of season close-out at Gadzooks, a mall store that is a favorite of teens. Carry-in dinners are fun, since teens like to cook, and it saves money if you only provide one dish instead of a whole meal.

THE COLLECTION CONNECTION

The lock-ins help you establish rapport with the teens because you are spending quality time with them and they appreciate it. This rapport is going to make you more approachable in the library, improving your service to the teens. Staff members that help at lock-ins will enjoy better communication with teens, which is good for the teens, good for the staff, good for the library, and good for the community. The teens meet new friends. The parties and lock-ins I have held supported reading program themes, volunteer projects, and featured games with questions about the library, books, authors, and librarians. These activities make the library a more familiar and comfortable place for teens to be.

TEEN FEEDBACK

- "As a finale for our summer reading program at the Coshocton Public Library, RoseMary planned a lock-in which was extremely fun! For the past three years, the library has been open after hours for one night in which activities were planned for us to enjoy. The activities usually dealt with the theme of the summer reading program. One year we played a "Live Clue" game, watched a movie, played games, and ate enjoyable foods. Another year, we played a Survivor game, had an auction with points we had accumulated from the game, ate and played other little games. This has become a fun and wonderful tradition that I participate in right before the busy time of school in August." Alison Jones
- "The Survivor theme of the lock-in was really neat! I had a great time and met some wonderful people. But, unfortunately, I wasn't the sole survivor." Amy Schlegel
- "The lock-ins were my favorite activity. Spending time with friends doing crazy activities and adding food into the equation makes a great combination." Andrea Sweitzer
- "I loved the Pizza Taste-Off. It was so cool playing the trivia game and eating pizza." Matt Shroyer
- "As a participant one year and a library employee helping the next, I enjoyed the Teen Lock-Ins. As a participant, I had much fun with all of the games and events, watching movies, and also hanging out with friends. As an employee helping out at a Lock-In, I had fun in a different way seeing all of the kids having a good time with smiles on their faces." Travis Walters

RESOURCES

Barrows, Roger E. 2001. *Recreation Handbook for Camp, Conference and Community.* Jefferson, North Carolina: McFarland & Company, Inc.

McCollan, Dan, and Keith Betts. 1992. *Junior High Game Nights: Wild and Crazy Outreach Events for Junior High Ministry.* Grand Rapids, Michigan: Zondervan Publishing House.

Chapter 10

Programs for Teens and Parents

OVERVIEW

Many libraries face annual requests from parents and students for science fair help and college information. These are two opportunities to bring parents and students together into the library for informative programs. Programs like Science Fair Help Day and College Knowledge help parents and students find information and support at the library and provide the opportunity to meet with other parents and students with similar questions and concerns.

Science Fair Help Day

The Science Fair Help Day is designed for students and their parents to come to the library to find project ideas, to see how science is at work in their community, and to gather information to complete a science fair project successfully. This program provides guidance for first-time science fair students, consolidates resources for experienced students, gives relief to parents, and provides educational fun for children.

The open-house style program has been held on a Sunday afternoon in January for two hours at our library for the past several years. Displays by local industries, the hospital, and the agricultural research station are arranged for viewing and manned by their own employees who volunteer their time to answer questions about their fields. Several students find mentors for their projects while asking questions at the display tables and their parents are also learning about the business and industries in their community.

Joel Moore, a local science teacher, has provided an interesting display about flight—a simple flight experiment for students to try that illustrates the scientific method—and has had homemade water rockets to show, as well as tips on what makes a good project. Models and instructions for paper airplanes on a table nearby provide a hands-on activity, and many planes take a test flight off the balcony.

Margaret Lowe, a retired reference librarian, has brought her rock, crystal, and gem collection for an interesting interactive display. Patrons could do their own excavating in a box of fossil-filled shale with nut picks and she had an activity to name all the minerals and gems she was wearing that day. Another year she brought a fascinating display called Nature's Papermakers— a collection of hornets nests of all sizes with a lot of information about bees, hornets, and wasps. One nest could be torn apart and students could take pieces of the paper home.

Figure 10–1 Science Fair Help Day Presenter.
Margaret is ready to share her amazing hornet nest collection with science fair students and their parents.

Ron Leeseberg, a local amateur astronomer, has made a homemade spectroscope and had an interesting display about stars and how astronomers determine the composition and distance of stars by their light. Another year he worked at a computer station helping students find interesting age-appropriate projects on a Scientific American CD he had brought with him. Another amateur astronomer brought a "sewer scope," a homemade telescope made with PVC pipe, with the instructions for building your own. It was set up to look at astronomy posters across the room.

Figure 10–2 Science Fair Help Day Presenter.
Ron Leeseberg helps students choose grade-level science projects that will interest them.

Several students on the Young Adult advisory board have loaned their science fair projects for display each year and speak with parents and students about their experiences. Two district science fair judges (who are parents of YA board members) volunteer their time to mingle and talk with the attendees about what is expected at a judging.

Two reference librarians are available to help with researching on the Internet and in books. The science fair books were available in special displays in the reference department and the children's room. Photocopies were free to science fair students for the afternoon.

A Mad Scientist Lab set up in the children's room invites families to explore hands-on activities and to view science curiosities, such as making crystals, rubber eggs, and looking through a microscope. One year there was a station to make your own slime to take home and another for bubble science. We also have had a working volcano. These activities are educational and fun and inspire students to begin working on their own projects. The lab also attracts younger siblings and their parents. Instructions are available so students can repeat the experiments at home. Diane Jones, the children's librarian, dressed in a lab coat, goggles, and pocket protector, is our Mad

Scientist and is aided by Sara Mesaros, the Kitchen Chemist, who wears an apron. Both are kept busy answering questions about the experiments.

Figure 10–3 Science Fair Help Day Kitchen Chemist.
Sara, the Kitchen Chemist, explains how to use the acid/base indicators in the Mad Scientist's Lab.

To coordinate a Science Fair Help Day, start planning early. Find out when the science fair projects are due in your county. Our schools all work on different schedules towards the county-wide science fair, so our date is a compromise. The help day should be at least several weeks before the projects are due.

To involve the community, write to local industries, utilities, medical businesses, and any other businesses you might have in your community that uses science in their processes. Explain the program and ask for their participation. Follow the letter with a phone call to the person you wrote to and ask who will be participating in the program from their company, then get direct contact information for that person. This is a great public relations opportunity for industries to show what they do for the community. Call your contact directly, explain the program, ask how they would like to participate, and ask for any special requirements they might have for their display, such as a computer or electrical outlets and adequate table space. You may need to make suggestions, such as posters illustrating processes, handouts, equipment used in their businesses, and so forth. Give them your contact information in case they have questions later.

Fax or write the science teachers in your schools telling them about the program you are planning and ask them if they would like to participate with a display or experiment or if they have suggestions for content. Give them a commitment date and your contact information. Other community members or staff members may have hobbies in a science field. Contact them with a letter and a follow-up phone call. A letter gives them time to think about the idea and think of possible displays or activities before your call.

To publicize the open house, make posters, flyers, or bookmarks for the schools to pass out to the students in the science classes. Our schools will take a master and make the copies. Advertise on the radio and in the newspaper. If you have a display case, fill it with borrowed lab equipment, science fair books, and an announcement for the upcoming program. One year I used portraits of famous scientists from the vertical file. Black paper on the bottom shelf of the case gives the case a lab table look. Marbles and colored water in flasks and beakers add color. Red and yellow cellophane made an effective flame on a Bunsen burner. Another year I divided the display case into different branches of science featuring books, science equipment, and natural artifacts: shells, fossils, hornet's nests, rocks. Put an ad in your library newsletter and make small posters for the shelves near the science fair books. Send an article to be read on morning announcements at school, or have one of your teens write and read one at his school.

Figure 10–4 Science Fair Help Day Mad Scientist Lab.
The Mad Scientist Lab has many hands-on science activities. This student is testing the properties of homemade slime and the crystal garden in the foreground waits to be examined with a magnifying glass. Instructions to reproduce the experiments are available to the students.

DETAILS TO COMPLETE THE PROGRAM

- A disk of bookmarks for science fair sites can be loaded on the public computers right before open house or when science fair season begins. The bookmarks can also be printed in a handout for students to take home.
- Make banners or tent cards for each display table to identify the participants and to help direct them when they come to set up.
- Make name tags for participants. I added a medallion with blue and gold ribbons to the name tags for extra flair.
- Offer books to display on each business's table in the scientific field they represent.
- Make a program flyer thanking the participants and noting all the displays, so nothing is overlooked by attendees.
- Make a directional sign by the entrance if you have activities in various parts of the library.
- Follow up with thank-you notes to everyone who helped.

IDEAS FOR PRESENTERS

- Science teachers: displays, talk to students and parents
- Science fair judges: talk to students and parents
- Hospital lab technicians: displays, lab equipment, microscope, and slides
- Medical professionals: displays
- Industries: displays, hands-on experiments
- Utilities: lab equipment, displays
- Agricultural research station: displays
- Recycling company: displays, hands-on experiments
- Science fair students: science fair projects, talk to parents and students
- YA board members: serve refreshments, pass out programs, help with lab experiments
- Amateur astronomers: displays, telescopes
- Red Cross: health and rescue displays and demonstrations
- Weatherman: displays
- Model rocketry enthusiast: rocket launch
- Fossil collector: displays, hands-on excavating

INSTRUCTIONS FOR MAD SCIENTIST LAB EXPERIMENTS

Display science fair books on the lab table so experimenters can check them out and learn more.

- Chemical reaction: Build a volcano around a baby bottle by crumpling plastic shopping bags to create a mountain shape around the bottle and taping them into place. Cover the mountain with papier mache made with white glue thinned with water and newspaper strips, leaving the mouth of the bottle open. Use tan tissue paper for the last outer layers. Let dry. The volcano may be painted, if desired. Spray the dry volcano with acrylic spray so it may be reused. To erupt the volcano: 1. Fill the bottle most of the way with water. 2. Add several drops of red food coloring. 3. Add 6 drops of dish detergent. 4. Add 2 T. baking soda. 5. Slowly pour in vinegar until the lava flows. When it slows down, add more vinegar. When the reaction stops, start over! Keep a bucket nearby to pour off lava.

- Density, floating eggs: Fill two glasses with the same amount of water. Add 2–3 T. salt to one glass and stir. Add an egg to each glass and observe. Carefully adding salt to the plain water containing the egg can result in an egg suspended midway in the water.
- Density rainbow: Pour small amounts of each of the following ingredients in separate containers: Karo, glycerin, water, rubbing alcohol, baby oil. Add drops of food coloring to all but the baby oil, coloring each ingredient a different color. Carefully pour the ingredients into a clear container, making sure they do not touch the sides of the container, in the following order: Karo, glycerin, water, alcohol, then baby oil last. A graduated cylinder makes a good container for this experiment and pouring the liquids down a glass rod may make it easier to keep them from becoming mixed. If there is a little mixing, it should settle and separate in a short time.
- Acid and base tester: Chop 1/4 head of red cabbage into small pieces, place in a saucepan. Cover with water and bring to a boil for five minutes. Let cool and strain, collecting the liquid in a jar. Dip both ends of cotton swabs in the liquid and let dry on a rack. The swabs are the indicators the students will use to test acids and bases. They will turn red in acids and blue in bases. Examples of liquids to test are ammonia, lemon juice, and vinegar. Baby food jars are convenient for the liquids. To use the indicator for revealing secret messages, write on a piece of paper with a clean swab dipped in lemon juice. Let dry. Rub a swab dipped in the indicator solution over the paper to reveal the invisible writing.
- Cartesian diver: Fill a soda bottle with room temperature water. Fill a glass with room temperature water and draw the water into an eyedropper until the dropper will float in the glass with its top barely above the surface. Transfer the eyedropper to the soda bottle without changing the water level in the dropper. Screw the cap onto the bottle tightly. Squeeze the bottle to make the diver sink, rise, or hover.

- Lava lamp: Pour about three inches of water into a jar. Pour about 1/3 cup of vegetable oil into the same jar. Add a drop or two of food coloring and observe. Shake salt on top of the oil for five seconds and observe. For the lab, I use a large beaker, fill it 2/3 full of water and pour about two inches of cooking oil on top and a few drops of red food coloring. The salt is in a small bowl nearby with a 1/8 t. measuring spoon in it, and a salt shaker is available for experimenting with different amounts of salt. The salt will be encased in a bubble of oil as it falls through the water. When it reaches the bottom, the oil breaks away and floats back to the top.
- Plaster of paris fossils: Cover a small shell or twig with petroleum jelly. Put 1/2 cup plaster of paris in a margarine dish. Add about 1/4 cup water and stir until thick and creamy. After the plaster hardens for a minute, press the shell or twig into the surface of the plaster and let it dry overnight. Remove the object. Plastic artificial leaves with veins also make good impressions.
- Silly slime: Mix one quart of water with 1/4 cup borax in a jar. Mix one cup Elmer's glue and one cup water in another jar and add food coloring; green is a good slime color. Shake well. To make slime, mix 2 T. borax solution with 6 T. glue solution and stir. Knead the slime with your hands until smooth. Store in a zip lock bag. One year we made a big batch and displayed it in a bowl for hands-on experimenting. Another year we let the kids mix their own slime in a paper cup and take it home in a baggie.
- Crystal garden: Whack charcoal or a brick into small bits or cut up a sponge and spread on a non-metal plate or tray. Spray with water until soaked. In a jar mix: 3 T. ammonia, 6 T. laundry bluing, 3 T. salt, and stir until dissolved. Pour over charcoal/sponge. Add 2 T. water to the jar to swirl out the rest of the chemicals and pour onto tray. Drop food coloring here and there, if desired. Sprinkle with 2 T. more salt. Set aside. On days two and three, pour a mixture of 2 T. ammonia, 2 T. water, and 2 T. bluing in the bottom of the tray. The crystals are fragile—provide a magnifying glass for a closer look.
- Rubber egg: Place an egg in a quart jar and cover with white vinegar. Change the vinegar the next day. Let soak for a week. Use a raw or boiled egg. I do two eggs, one soaking and one in a bowl that is already rubberized for touching. Try soaking a chicken bone, it will become flexible.
- Alum crystal: Heat one cup water to boiling. Stir in 3 T. alum. Pour into jar and cover with plastic wrap. Let set for several days. One large crystal should form.

- Mold garden: Collect moldy foods from co-workers or grow your own. Provide a magnifying glass for examining. To grow mold, sprinkle a piece of bread with water and let stand for about an hour. Place in a jar with a lid. Put in a warm dark place for a few days.
- Colored celery: Partially split a stalk of celery from the bottom. Place each half of the stalk in separate containers (two paper cups beside each other works). Add water to both cups and add red food coloring to one cup and blue to the other. In a few hours the leaf veins of the celery will show the colors.
- Egg in a bottle: Find a milk bottle with a top that is slightly smaller than a shelled hard-cooked egg. Wad up a small piece of paper, light it with a match, drop it into the bottle and allow it to burn out. Place the egg on top of the bottle and it will go in. To get the egg out, turn the bottle upside-down and blow into it very hard.
- Microscope: Use a microscope with an electric light. Use prepared labeled slides. We borrow a microscope from the water treatment plant and use prepared slides from a child's microscope set.

THE BOTTOM LINE

The biggest expense of this program is the time spent planning it. The day of the program is almost effortless after the Mad Scientist Lab is set up. A committee could make shorter work of planning everything by sharing the job of writing letters, making phone calls, and planning the lab. We serve refreshments, punch, and cookies provided by the Friends, with a cost of about $30.00. Most of the ingredients for the lab come from my kitchen or the library kitchen.

THE COLLECTION CONNECTION

Science fair experiment books, science reference books, Science Fair on File experiments, Science Fair Index, science fair Internet sites. Display science books near the lab tables, on display tables, and in the reference area.

College Knowledge

This program for college bound high school students and their parents showcases what the library has to offer to assist in the college selection and application process. Two staff members can share this presentation, one speaking about the books and the other about the Internet and other electronic resources. Packets are passed out to the students with a notepad, pencil, the Site-Seeing Tour for College Bound Students handout (see Figures 10–5 and 10–6), a bibliography of college related materials, various calendars, schedules, and checklists for college planning.

The Internet can save you time and money when you prepare for college entrance exams, take campus tours, apply to colleges, or search for financial aid!

Test Prep

www.achieva.com
Achieva.com offers Online SAT I, SAT II, PSAT and ACT Test Prep, Online College Admissions Prep, and Online Study Skills

www.kaplan.com
Kaplan offers test preparation and admissions information

www.collegeboard.com
The College Board offers practice tests, test dates, online test registration for the SAT, and online college application links

www.princetonreview.com
The Princeton Review offers practice tests, guidance, and tutoring

Test Tip: Familiarize yourself with all SAT test instructions before exam day. It is a waste of time to read them during the test itself!

Campus Tours

www.collegeview.com
CollegeView® Virtual Tours include multi-media virtual tours, audio clips, InfoZap® electronic mail, and hot links to colleges' home pages

www.icollege.com
iCollege offers virtual tours of hundreds of colleges

www.criterioninfo.net/vcd/control.html
College Essentials offers many links to college tours and college homepages

Figure 10–5 College Site-Seeing Tour Page 1.
Site-Seeing Tour for college bound students: create a take-home pamphlet with Web sites that will guide the students and their parents through the college application process.

The guests are seated around a rectangular table arrangement to make note taking and book browsing comfortable. Reference and circulating books about the college preparation process are arranged by subject on a book cart in the following order: test preparation, college handbooks, choosing a school, the application process, scholarships and financial aid, campus life. The contents are briefly explained and a few of the books are passed around the tables.

Following the book presentation, the Site Seeing Tour guide and CD-ROM

Choosing Schools

www.collegeview.com
Choose colleges by: Major, Public/Private, Two or Four Year, Location by State, City Size, Men's Athletics, Student Body Type, Women's Athletics, Student Body Size, Co-ed Athletics, Religious Affiliation, Disabilities, Special Services, Ethnic Mix

www.embark.com
Embark's Matchmaker asks a series of questions to match you with the right school

Applications

www.embark.com
Embark will send your one application to many colleges at once and offers advice and checklists

www.review.com
Simultaneous applications also available here by filling out one form

TIP: In some cases you pay a lower application fee if you apply online!

Scholarships/Financial Aid

www.fafsa.ed.gov
The FAFSA form is available and easier to complete online

www.fastweb.com
FastWeb will match your interests to over 500,000 scholarships and has loan calculators and comparisons

TIP: Most college sites have chat rooms and bulletin boards where you can get to know classmates before landing on campus!

Figure 10–6 College Site-Seeing Tour Page 2.

products are presented as alternatives and supplements to the books. The total speaking time is limited to a half hour. A general question and answer period follows. The group is then dismissed to browse the books, ask individual questions, and browse the Internet using the Site-Seeing Tour guide. Circulating items are available for checkout.

THE BOTTOM LINE

This program doesn't have to cost anything, but you can add refreshments, door prizes, or freebies if you have something suitable. We offered college mugs, pennants, or stationery for the students, and cider and donuts for refreshments.

THE COLLECTION CONNECTION

ACT, SAT, PSAT preparation books and CDs, college guides, how to get scholarships, how to write college essays, FAFSA forms, college prep videos, and college Web sites.

International Game Night

International Game Night is for the whole family. We held our International Game Night during the Where in the World Are You Reading? summer reading program on a Friday evening after hours. We had received a Fatherhood Initiative grant from the Family and Children First Council in our county. They donated parenting books to be given to all the fathers who attended and pool passes for their families. We spent the grant money on food for the evening.

Game tables were set up in the adult, children's, and teen rooms of the library with age appropriate games in each area. International refreshments were served in the meeting room where geography bingo was played. Board games were borrowed from staff members and hopscotch squares were taped out on the floor. A piñata party in the parking lot ended the evening. Children were blindfolded and given a chance to swing at the piñata in order of age, from youngest to oldest. When the piñata breaks, stand back for the stampede!

The refreshments in the meeting room were tacos in a bag, Chinese spring rolls, sweet and sour chicken, pizza, and fortune cookies. The pizza, chicken, and spring rolls were from local restaurants and we made the tacos in a bag. Soda in cans were self-serve.

Tacos in a bag is a fun snack for any teen event. Prepare taco filling and keep warm in a crock pot. Chop tomatoes and onions and place in separate bowls with spoons. Grate cheddar cheese or buy it already grated and place in another bowl with a spoon. Shred lettuce and place in bowl with tongs. Provide a jar of taco sauce and a container of sour cream with spoons. To serve, crush a small snack size bag of Doritos and open the top. Add a spoon of taco filling and let your guests add other toppings as desired. Serve with a plastic fork to eat right out of the bag.

Several teens came to the event with a parent and some of the TAB members assisted with the children's games. I taught several boys how to play Mancala and we had Parcheesi, Chinese Checkers, and several other board games in the teen area.

THE BOTTOM LINE

All the games were borrowed from staff members or owned by the YA department. The food and the piñata were the main expenses. The piñata cost about $10 and was filled with small wrapped candies. The food cost approximately $200.00 including plates, napkins, and beverages. Since this program incorporated all ages, staff members from several departments helped with serving food and manning the game areas.

TEEN FEEDBACK

• "Science Fair Help Day has always been an important and fun event—both to those helping and those coming. It has given many people ideas and very good advice from actual science fair judges." Amy Schlegel

RESOURCES

Bizarre Stuff You Can Make in Your Kitchen [Online]. Available: http://www.geocities.com/molerat 1964 [2002, July 31].

Honnold, RoseMary. *Science Fair Links* [Online]. Available: www.cplrmh.com/sciencelinks.html [2002, May 10].

Smith, Tammy. 1998. "Science Fair Help Day." *VOYA* (February): 373.

Chapter 11

Programs for Teens and Children

OVERVIEW

Programming across the generations is a wonderful experience for the teens and for the audience. The teens appreciate the opportunity to share and entertain and the children enjoy seeing and working with the teens.

Reader's Theater

Reader's Theater is a story in which the characters' parts are read by different people. Participation is not so stressful since memorization and great acting skills are not required. Few rehearsals are required, which makes it a little easier to work into teens' already busy schedules. Props are optional, but the teens like making them and the audience likes seeing them. Cartoon-like props made from poster board, paint, and markers are perfect for a children's production, or the actual objects can be used. The teens enjoy making the children laugh and the children think the teens are just great. Some skits are adaptable to audience participation.

Six teens from our YA group presented "In Which Tigger Comes to the Forest and Has Breakfast" to an audience of 31 children to celebrate Winnie the Pooh's 75th birthday. The script came from *Presenting Reader's Theater: Plays and Poems to Read Aloud* by Caroline Feller Bauer. There are many other scripts already prepared in this book suitable for a child audience.

The teens read the script round robin style at a TAB meeting, each teen reading a line so we could hear the entire story. The teens were then asked who would like to participate in presenting this play to the children. The whole group helped cast the roles after they experimented a little with expressions and voices.

Practices were sketchy since it was nearly impossible to get everyone there at the same time. Our only practice with everyone there together was an hour before the presentation, but that worked just fine. The two other practices were spent on making some props from poster board and working out the logistics of coming in, deciding where everyone needed to stand, how Tigger was going to move through the scenes, and how to end the play.

We presented the play as the first part of an hour long birthday party program. After the play, which took approximately 15 minutes, the children were divided into four groups, each named for a Pooh character, and each group rotated through four different activity centers. They decorated bear cutout cookies and had punch, they played action games (Pooh Sticks, Hot Potato with a stuffed bee puppet, and a Kanga and Roo jumping game). They watched a Pooh video while coloring Pooh pictures, and they played a memory game and word search. The teens helped the children with all of these activities.

The teens were excited to try Reader's Theater and asked to do it again. The children in the audience laughed at the right places and remained attentive through the story. Several of the children told the teens they really liked the play and told them "they did a really good job."

Our next Reader's Theater presentation was two African folk tales for an arts festival program. The scripts were found on Aaron Shepherd's Web site. The skits we used were "The Calabash Kids" and "How Frog Went to Heaven." I rewrote "The Calabash Kids" so we could use children from the audience as the calabash gourd children. Once again our props were simple, constructed of poster board. A flat box decorated as a fireplace for one play flipped over to be a well for the next and became the focus for center stage. The program began with "The Calabash Kids" and then the children made a craft that was a shape of a gourd to which they drew a face, added googly eyes, yarn hair, and glued on accordion folded arms and legs. This gave the teens time to switch the scenery, change props, and orient themselves for the next play. After presenting "How Frog Went To Heaven," the children created frogs from green paper plates. The teens gathered props, snacked on cookies, and were free to go. The whole program took about an hour. The children's librarian and her assistant arranged for the crafts and refreshments for the children.

Figure 11–1 Reader's Theater Cast.
The cast and crew of "The Calabash Kids" prepare to take a bow.

THE BOTTOM LINE

All of the props for these plays were made with materials available at the library. The children's department took care of the crafts and snacks for the children. The teens did go through a package of cookies afterward!

Medieval Festival

The teens were a big part of the Medieval Festival that celebrated the end of our Medieval Summer Reading Program. Teens served food, painted faces, wrapped and braided hair, managed games, supervised sidewalk chalk painting, and had painted appliance boxes for the games. A refrigerator box was painted to look like a castle tower for the game, Fish in the Moat. Children went fishing by tossing a line with a clothespin on the end over the castle tower wall. They each caught a prize that was attached to their clothespin hook by a teen hiding in the box. A dragon with a big mouth was painted on a dryer box. A hole was cut in his mouth. This game was called Feed the Dragon and the children tossed bean bags into the dragon's mouth to win a prize. All the children received tickets to attend the fair and had to present a ticket at each activity so everyone had a chance to participate and earn prizes.

Figure 11–2 Medieval Fair Hair Wrapping.
Teens were kept busy braiding and making hair wraps for the children at the Medieval Fair.

The Society for Creative Anachronisms came and performed sword fights, which the teens enjoyed watching. A strolling minstrel provided music and sang ballads. Sir Roger presented an entertaining program for the whole family in full armor on the hottest day of the year! He was a fun and interesting speaker.

Contact information for Sir Roger:

Roger McKinney
Segami Studio

Figure 11–3 Medieval Fair Fishing in the Moat.
**Teens painted the castle tower for the fishing game and a dragon
for the bean bag toss. All of these activities wouldn't have been
possible without the help of the Teen Advisory Board members. (See
Figure 11–3.)**

82 West Main Street
Shelby, OH 44875–1206
419–347–6340
e-mail: segami@bright.net
FEE: Contact performer for current fee.

Another guest wrote children's names in fancy calligraphy on cards. She
had a simple setup with a card table, cards in various colors, and pens. Guests
could give her a ticket to write their names in calligraphy.

The food table had a list of Medieval table manners posted and tent cards
labeling such delicious treats as Dragon Toes (cocktail wieners in barbeque
sauce), Love Knots (big pretzels), Castle Rubble (snack mix), and Dragon
Juice (green punch).

Carnival

A circus theme for summer reading suggests a carnival event. Teens can man the games, dress as clowns, paint faces, build props, and serve food. Rent or borrow a popcorn wagon, a cotton candy machine, a sno-cone machine, and cook hotdogs on a grill. Ask the teens if they or their friends can juggle, ride a unicycle, or do gymnastics. If the event is held in a park, a shelter can be decorated like a circus tent and activities can be arranged in rings. Games can depend on the weather. Water games are fun when it is hot, and more active games when it is cooler. Schools or churches may lend their carnival games. The links below have many ideas for games and activities to create with your teens for a family carnival.

THE BOTTOM LINE

These end of summer events are usually the big investment for the library's summer programming budget. Food, guest speakers, activities, and props all vary in cost. Teen volunteers really add to the fun of the afternoon with the games and activities they build and provide. They can help brainstorm ideas, volunteer activities and talents, and donate materials. They add energy to the whole event.

TEEN FEEDBACK

- "For one of the children's parties the YA group performed a Pooh play. None of us could act, but I think that made the experience that much more fun." Andrea Sweitzer
- "I enjoyed this event [Medieval Fair] a lot as a helper representing the Teen Advisory Board. This event was mostly for the children and included games, food, and other fun activities. My job was to help with a game. I had a good time because I could tell the kids were having a good time." Travis Walters

RESOURCES

Bauer, Caroline Feller. 1987. *Presenting Reader's Theater: Plays and Poems to Read Aloud.* New York: H.W. Wilson.

Shepherd, Aaron. *Aaron Shepherd's RT Page* [Online]. Available: www.aaronshep.com/rt/index.html [2002, May 11].

Talk of the Town [Online]. Available: www.tottevents.com/themeparties/ [2002, May 11].

Chapter 12

Field Trips

OVERVIEW

A few years ago the Teen Advisory Board asked to go on a field trip. It seemed a tall order at the time since our community is fairly small and most local areas of interest are toured by students during their school time. The trip needed to have a connection to the library or reading or books to make it worthwhile and to fit into my idea of our purpose as a group. I cannot recall how it all came together, but the result was a shopping trip to a bookstore where the teens could choose books for the YA room.

The Borders Shopping Trip

The Borders Shopping Trip has become a favorite annual program for the Teen Advisory Board. Our nearest Borders store is an hour away so we take a day trip on a Saturday in March. We leave at 9 a.m., shop until lunch time, have lunch, and return to the library about 3:00–3:30 p.m.

During the February TAB meeting before the trip we go the YA room and make shopping lists. The teens look at the collection and see what areas they think we need to add newer or more books, music, and graphic novels. They also look at what magazine subscriptions we have so they can look over the magazines at Borders for ideas for new subscriptions. I make a note of any classics that need to be replaced or added. Teens interested in completing a series write down which ones we need, or if it is a subject area they are interested in building up, they make note of what we already have. The lists are tools to encourage the teens to take a good look at the collection and think about what they would like to add so they will have something in mind before they get to the store. There is also some impulse shopping, which is fun, because they always find books I haven't seen in the reviews. Encourage them to think about buying books their friends would like, too.

The Friends of the Library pay for our lunch. They also make donations towards the book purchases, but we also use the YA book budget. Borders has given us a corporate discount, we aren't paying shipping, and I am buying what the teens are going to read, so it is a good use of the book budget. We take the library credit card and a tax exempt form. A few of my co-workers car pool the teens to the store with me and their mileage is paid by the library. The teens all must have a permission slip signed by a parent or guard-

---

Coshocton Public Library
Teen Advisory Board
Field Trip

On March 9, 2002, our YA Board will have the opportunity to go on a field trip to Borders Bookstore in Canton, Ohio (330-494-4776). This will be a shopping trip sponsored by the Friends of the Library, and all of the Teen board members may choose books for the Teen collection at the library!

Borders is a huge bookstore with a great variety of books and music and also has a coffee shop and the Old Navy Store is next door. The teens are welcome to bring their own shopping money, but the focus of the trip is to buy books for the YA department. The books will have a bookplate showing who chose the book for the collection.

Our plan is to leave by 9 a.m. and arrive at the store about 10:15 a.m. We will do our tour and book shopping first, then after some personal shopping time, have lunch nearby, also sponsored by the Friends. We plan to return to the library by 3:30-4:00 p.m. We will be carpooling and only adult library employees will be driving.

I need to have a signed permission slip for EACH YA member under 18 years of age who will be accompanying us on our Field Trip. Please return to me ASAP, and let me know by phone or e-mail by Friday March 1st, if you are going so I can coordinate drivers.
RoseMary Honnold
YA Coordinator
622-0956
honnolro@oplin.lib.oh.us

Permission Slip for YA Field Trip to Borders

I give my permission for _____
to accompany the Teen Advisory Board on the Shopping Trip to Borders bookstore in Canton, Ohio on March 9, 2002.

Signature of parent or guardian _____

Figure 12–1 Borders Shopping Trip Permission Slip.
A permission slip explains the details of the trip to the teens and their parents or guardians.

ian. It is sent home at the February meeting and has to be returned a few days before the trip so I can finalize riding arrangements.

While we are shopping, I keep a book cart with me, a pad of Post-It notes, a calculator, and a few pencils. The teens are each given a dollar amount to spend. Some of them decide to buy something special and spend all of their portion on a couple of books, while others shop for bargains to get the most for their money. When they have a dollar or two left, groups pool their funds to buy one more item. After someone chooses his books, he brings them to me, I stick a Post-It in it with his name on it and place it on the cart. The Post-It stays with the book until after processing at the library so I can make a bookplate for it. When everyone is finished shopping or I think we have spent enough money, I take the cart to the checkout. After the teens ooh and ahh over how much money we've spent, we go outside, and pose for a picture with the books and the very long sales slip!

Figure 12–2 Borders Shopping Trip.
The Borders Shopping Trip has become an annual favorite program for the TAB.

At the library, all the books are processed and returned to me. I make the bookplates with MS Publisher on cardstock and glue them to the inside covers. The bookplate has the name of the teen that chose the book and the date of the trip. That teen has first chance to check out the book at the next meeting. A list of their purchases and the group photo are put on display in the YA room with the new books as they are returned. Most of the books are checked out within two weeks. The teens enjoy coming in and seeing their purchases checked out.

The Friends like to see what the teens have chosen, so plan to take a few of the books to their next meeting and share photos with them to help keep the funding for the trip in the budget from year to year.

Other Field Trip Ideas

A trip to a bindery or a publishing house would give teens a behind-the-scenes look into book making. These trips introduce new ideas for career choices to the teens. A trip to a university library or large metropolitan library would impress upon them the amazing amount of books available to them, especially if your library is a small one. A trip to another library to meet with their TAB would be a fun and enlightening experience for all. Discussing their activities and looking at each other's YA collections would give them great ideas for future planning meetings. Take scrapbooks and photo albums to share. Look at the resources in your area and plan a field trip for your teens soon!

THE BOTTOM LINE

The Friends budget about $200.00 for the Borders trip. That is enough for lunch for everyone, including the drivers, and a few books. The amount you spend on books depends on your budget and collection, but anything the teens pick out will be checked out at least once! The discount Borders gives us, plus not paying shipping, makes up for the gas money spent getting us there and back. Our work schedules are adjusted that week so we don't run into extra staff hours. The experience is priceless!

TEEN FEEDBACK

- "Wow! The Borders trips have always been a blast. The best part is getting to have our say as to what books are going to get added to the YA collection. Plus, it's kind of neat to pick up a book and see that it was chosen by someone your age." Amy Schlegel
- "The Borders trip gave me the opportunity to pick out books and music for the YA room." Andrea Sweitzer
- "The teens in the TAB went to Canton to the Borders Bookstore. We got to pick out different books that we liked for the library. We got first pick on the books we chose. All of us got in a group and had our picture taken." Mellonee Hook
- "Every year, the YA Board goes on a trip to Borders. Our Friends of the Library gave us money to buy books for the YA room. After getting a tour of the bookstore, we picked out books for the library and then shopped for ourselves. After the book buying, we went out to lunch at Cracker Barrel and departed for home." Alison Jones

- "I liked the trip to the Borders Book Store in Canton, Ohio. My favorite part included looking around at the store for about two hours picking out books for the young adult section at the Coshocton Public Library. Going out to eat after shopping was really fun, which included visiting with friends, having good food and lots of laughs." Travis Walters

Chapter 13

Teen Volunteer Programs

OVERVIEW

Teens can perform many tasks at the library that will save the staff time and help make programs more complete. Volunteering gives the teens a good sense of purpose in the library, as many of these tasks may not get done and some programs couldn't happen without them.

If your library has a TAB, some of the volunteer work can be done at the meetings. Our group has often cut out, folded, assembled, sorted, and stapled while discussing books and programs at our meetings. A sign-up sheet can be passed around for other volunteer projects that must be completed at other times. Explain the date and time and what the job entails and ask the teens to write their phone numbers down to be contacted for a reminder.

While our TAB is also a volunteer group, some libraries organize a Volunteen Group. Their task is to be available to help do routine and special event jobs around the library that will save staff time. Some school districts require volunteer hours for graduation. The library documents the time a teen has volunteered for credit. Volunteering in the community also looks good on college applications. Teens may need you to document time or sign applications for them when they apply to colleges.

Even without a TAB or an organized Volunteen group, you can involve teens with a job jar or job file. A file of volunteer projects that includes instructions for each job, a space for a date when the job is completed, and the name of the person who performed the task can be kept at the main desk. When a teen drops in with some free time, a volunteer opportunity is waiting for him.

The level of commitment and seriousness with which the teens perform the volunteer jobs depends upon your commitment to match up the right teens with the right jobs. An application, interview, and training sessions can help you get to know the teens. Explaining task requirements and how the task fits in with the workings of the library will help them see the importance of their work.

Volunteer Jobs for Teens

- Dust shelves, read and straighten shelves, weed paperbacks, help select books and music, reinforce paperbacks and comics, add genre labels.
- Summer reading sign ups, Internet sign ups, help at children's programs with crafts, prepare crafts, decorate meeting room for children's parties, assemble summer reading packets, help at library programs by counting attendance, serving refreshments or ushering, setting up and cleaning up.
- Set up book displays, decorate bulletin boards, straighten the YA room, assemble photo albums, deliver newsletters and flyers to schools, record radio spots, read for radio story times, read to children in Book Buddy programs or story time programs.
- Help at the Friends book sales, make holiday cards for homebound patrons, wrap gifts and prizes.
- Large programs, like medieval fairs, Olympics, and carnivals would not be possible without teen volunteers at our library. They have painted

Figure 13–1 Teen Volunteers.
These teens all helped with a children's Valentine's Day program. They read stories, played games, served refreshments, and helped clean up afterwards.

faces, braided and woven hair, helped children with games, and served refreshments.

Figure 13–2 Teen Volunteers.
Teens assemble blue ribbon awards at a TAB meeting for a Reading Olympics program.

Tips for Creating Good Volunteers

- Introduce the teens to staff members and give them a behind-the-scenes tour of the library to make them feel a part of things.
- Match teens' interests and talents to the tasks.
- Teach them new skills.

- Train them to do the job correctly and have written instructions available as a checklist reminder.
- Communicate with staff, asking for jobs they need done and introduce them to the teen volunteers.
- Show appreciation to the teens for jobs well done.
- Be encouraging, listen, and maintain a sense of humor!

Rewards for Volunteers

Volunteers can be rewarded with a special party to show the library's appreciation. You may consider sharing a few library employee perks, such as first dibs on new books, choose a new book for the collection, or no fines. It is a good idea to keep a record of volunteer hours and jobs completed for statistics to present to the director to justify the existence of the group. If the teen needs time documented for job or college applications, this record is ready.

Certificates stating the number of volunteer hours served make a nice reward for the teens to keep in a scrapbook. A smile and a thank you in person is the most important way to show appreciation.

How to Organize a Teen Advisory Board

Teens are the BEST resource for finding out what your library can do for them. Don't waste time producing a program YOU think is a great idea but find out teens won't come to it! Let them help you plan and produce the program. Teens are our future financial supporters. Give them some lasting memories of good library experiences and they will be there for us in the future. Teens need to be heard and will become your friends and allies if you listen to them.

Invite teens (ages 12–19) that are already in the library, congregating after school or hanging around during the summer reading, using the Internet, doing homework, or checking out music or comics, to meet with you. Ask the school librarians for likely candidates from the teens that are active in their libraries. Some libraries choose a board for a defined period of time, others have casual groups that any interested teen can attend. If you opt for a fixed membership each year, give teens application forms and choose those you want to work with. Put up a poster in your teen area, make flyers for the checkout desk, send an announcement to be read at the schools, place applications in teen traffic areas, talk to the teens in your library. Try an interest survey in your teen area if you need feedback to begin.

The number of teens depends on how many you can work with comfortably, but keep in mind that every teen will not attend every meeting. For example, I have an average of twenty active teens each year, but most meetings have between nine and sixteen in attendance. Send meeting reminder postcards each month to your board members and include a topic or event that will be covered at the meeting.

You do not have to have a YA librarian to start a teen board! Our board was organized by four of us on staff that were interested in starting some teen programming. The interest generated by the board and the programs that resulted evolved into a need for a YA librarian who now manages the group.

A Teen Advisory Board can do many of the volunteer projects listed above. They can also help you develop the teen collection and a teen space. Let them choose music CDs, comics, magazines, and books, help weed paperbacks, straighten and read shelves, make displays, and decorate for holidays. They can plan teen programs and brainstorm ideas with you. Sign them up to help set up, clean up, publicize, provide refreshments, and make props.

Promote librarianship at TAB meetings: invite staff as guest speakers to tell what they do at the library. Start each meeting with book talks. Our teens sign up to be responsible for a book talk at a meeting. The rest of the teens are invited to share any titles they have enjoyed after the talk. I like to share any YA books that have received particular mention on the listservs, award winners, and my favorites, too. Eat and have fun together.

You can join a listserv, Teen Advisory Groups—Advisory Discussion (TAGAD-L), which is a discussion forum for the advisors of any public library teen advisory group. Send an e-mail to tagad-l-subscribe@topica.com to join. The listserv shares ideas and questions; a helpful resource and support group for YA librarians.

Work out meeting times with your teens. Try an hour or so after school, but before dinner, sports practices, and homework begin. The last Monday of each month, 4:00–5:00 p.m. works well for our library. Saturdays may work in your area. When scheduling evening programs for teens, keep in mind ballgames, music competitions, and practices.

Make an agenda of items that need to be covered before each meeting, allowing for discussion, visiting, and brainstorming. If your teens are from several different schools, this is a good thing, and you need to allow opportunity for them to visit with each other and get to know each other so they can work together. Ask the teens if they want officers. Our group opted to take turns each month. A sign-up sheet goes around a couple times each year to volunteer to lead the meeting, take the minutes, or give a book talk. Other groups prefer a more formal meeting. Let the teens decide what works for them.

Coshocton Public Library
Teen Advisory Board Application (for grades 7-12)
Questions? Call the library at 622-0956 and ask for RoseMary

Please fill out the following information and return to the main desk by September 14, 2001.

NAME _____ AGE _____

ADDRESS _____

PHONE _____ E-MAIL _____

SCHOOL _____ GRADE _____

Help me get to know you!

What are some of your hobbies and interests and other activities?

Tell me about your favorite book:

What are some of the books you have read lately that you enjoyed?

Tell me why you would like to be on the Teen Advisory Board:

_____
I am aware that my child is applying for a position on the Teen Advisory Board:
Signature of Parent or Guardian: _____

Figure 13–3 Teen Advisory Board Application.
    Make copies of the application form for the Teen Advisory Board available at the library and school libraries. Send copies to school librarians who may choose likely candidates.

Chapter 14

Publicity

OVERVIEW

Telling the right teens about the right program is all you have to do! Simple? Not at all. The traditional ways we publicize events through newspaper and radio may not work with teens in your area. Without abandoning those two avenues, adding other methods aimed particularly at teens are necessary.

The teens that come to your library regularly can be informed with displays, posters, bulletin boards, bookmarks, and flyers. These should be clear, directed towards teens, and look exciting with use of bright colors and hip, not juvenile, clip art. A monthly calendar of events should be posted in the YA room. The teen that visits sporadically or infrequently may be tougher to catch, not because he isn't interested in the program, but because he isn't in the library during your promotion. When I conducted a survey about the programs we had held during the year, the answer I saw most often is, "I would have come, but I didn't hear about it!" I immediately started rethinking the publicity the library currently used and how it worked (or didn't work) for teens.

E-Mail List

One way to help teens stay informed is building an e-mail list. Forms to join the list can be picked up in the YA room anytime. When teens are added to the list, they can receive regular e-mails from you that fill them in on all the upcoming events. The e-mails can also include lists of new books and music as they are added to the collection (annotated by the TAB), Web sites they may find helpful for homework or entertainment, or surveys about their interests. Adding your director, PR person, and the school librarians to the list will keep them informed about upcoming events as well. The same e-mail newsletter is also posted on our library Web site to keep the upcoming events up to date. BCC: all the e-mail addresses to protect everyone's privacy and to prevent anyone spamming the list. The e-mails are more informal (and cheaper) than a printed newsletter and the teens like receiving mail that is informative and directed towards them. Some of the teens may choose to communicate with you through e-mail after receiving one from you, suggesting titles or giving feedback about programs. The e-mail database can be expanded whenever you have a drawing, a contest, or a program by including a space on the entry slips for e-mail addresses. I maintain two e-mail lists, one for the TAB group and a general one for any teen that signs up. Sending out an e-mail takes very little time and you will reach many of the teens who have come to programs before and who use the YA room. I collect the forms and enter all the new addresses right before writing and sending an e-mail. Any addresses that bounce back are removed from the list the following day.

Join the YA E-mail List!
Receive 2 e-mails a month to keep you up to date on what's happening at the library for teens!

Name_____

Age_____

E-mail address_____

Return this slip to the reference desk.

Figure 14–1 E-Mail Sign Up.
Display these forms in the YA room and pass them out at every program. Writing one e-mail newsletter will keep all your active teens informed.

Newsletters

YA newsletters are another way to keep teens informed. The YA librarian can write all of it or accept articles from teens, or turn the content over to the TAB or a group of volunteer teens entirely. A newsletter does take time to put together. Articles need to be written, edited, and typed in a presentable format. The newsletters then need to be proofed, printed, and distributed. An online version can be added to the library's Web site, which would involve the library's Webmaster.

A TAB can help with most of these steps. For a brainstorming session at a TAB meeting, I passed around YA newsletters collected from several libraries. I asked the teens to look them over and tell me what they liked about them, articles they liked, and any ideas that came to mind while reading them. I wrote all of these ideas on a flip chart. After we had a full page of ideas, I asked them which one would each of them like to write about. I wrote their names by the article ideas and asked them to bring an article to the next meeting. I confirmed their commitments by a follow up e-mail that listed all the article topics and who signed up for them.

Deciding on a title for the newsletter and a layout was the next step for the group. Once again the flip chart was used as the teens generated a list of possible titles for the newsletter. After several suggestions were made, we voted on each, with the majority vote choosing the title. Next, we designed the layout of the front page. A calendar to list upcoming events, a table of contents, and feature articles about the upcoming programs were chosen and sketched out on the flip chart. The teens help arrange the rest of the newsletter in the same way.

A desktop publishing program is very helpful. My current favorite is MS Publisher, but there are others available, such as PageMaker. You can save typing time by asking the teens to e-mail the articles to you. Then copy and paste them into the text boxes and edit as needed. Original artwork and poetry are great additions. Artwork can be scanned and saved as a file and imported into the publication. Artwork looks better if the artist creates it in the size needed for the paper. Cartoons with conversation balloons can become unreadable if reduced too much to fit on a page. Teens familiar with the publishing software can help with copy fitting and editing.

The teens can distribute the newsletters by taking them to school to pass out among their friends and teachers, to share at the school library or English classrooms, to church youth groups, and to their other hangouts. Copies should also be available at the library. Send copies to the local newspapers and radio station to keep them informed of what is happening for teens at the library. Leave some at the main desk for the parents to pick up for their busy teens.

Suggested Articles for the First Issue	Assigned Writer
Video game review	Adam, Nate
Calendar of events	RoseMary
Monthly survey	Dusty, Rusty
TAB introductions	Misty, Mellonee
Books to movies review	Andrea, Mamie
Movie reviews	Alison
Mystery drawing	
Weird facts	Jared
Original poetry	
Web site review	Kristen, Kayla
YA book review	RoseMary
Electronic gadget review	Lanny
Role Playing Club report	Rachel
This month in history	Matthew
Jokes and riddles	Amy
Quotes	Amy

Figure 14–2 Newsletter Article List.
The teens can generate a list of article ideas at a TAB meeting. Go through the list and ask for volunteers to write the articles. Follow up the meeting with an e-mail reminder of assignments and deadlines.

Suggested Titles	# Votes
Libr@ry Connections	0
TeenLibr@ry Connections	0
YA Journal	1
Library Chronicles	2
YA Gazette	0
YAnonymous	1
Teen Zone	0
YA Today	everyone
Teen Opus	0
Teen Times	0
Teen Chronicles	1
For Teens By Teens	3
4TNS	3
Teen Tribute	1
Teen Scene	1

Figure 14–3 Newsletter Title List.
Teens feel ownership and pride publishing a newsletter in a group effort. After brainstorming a list of titles, they voted unanimously for "YA Today" as the title of their newsletter.

Display Case

The YA department claims the display case for the month of October to celebrate teens in the library. Using the ALA Teen Read Week theme, I feature the TAB members and all the programs we have done in the past year. Photos of TAB members and teens at programs always attract teen patrons to the display. The Teen Read Week main event program is also advertised in the display and books and props are added to go with the theme.

A photo session is planned for the TAB meeting in September. The members are photographed with books and props to go with the theme of Teen Read Week. The photos are used for the display and then given to the teens at the next meeting for their scrapbooks. Our library policy requires a photo release form to be signed by guardians of the models under 18, and those over 18 may sign their own. The forms are kept on file. For the teens' safety, I never post last names with their photos.

I hereby grant to the Coshocton Public Library and anyone authorized by the organization the right to copyright, reproduce, publish, and otherwise use my photograph and my name in all media, for purposes of advertising and promoting libraries and literacy.

Name/Age (Print)

_____

Signature

_____

Address

_____

Phone Number

_____

Date

_____

Witness (Parent or guardian if under 18)

_____

Figure 14–4 Photo Release.
Keep a file of signed photo release forms so photos can be used for displays and publicity in print or on the Internet.

Figure 14–5 Display Case.
A photo session at a TAB meeting is a lot of fun. Rachel is posing with a few of the medieval and fantasy props we collected for the "Make Reading a Hobbit" Teen Read Week theme.

Schools

Schools provide a captive audience for publicity about programs. Submit an article to the school newspaper or a teen on the newspaper staff may do a story about the library, programs, or the YA librarian. Programs can be promoted on the morning announcements. I fax a program poster to the schools for this purpose. Call the school office to find out who should receive the publicity flyers so they will be read on the announcements. TAB members may be willing to write and read an announcement. If you can arrange a visit to a classroom for book talks, do an ad for your programs enlisting any students that you know in the class. Promote programs in displays at career days, diversity days, and during card sign ups. Provide publicity posters for the cafeteria and school library.

Word of Mouth

Some of the best publicity for your library's programs will be among the teens by word of mouth. If they come to a program and have a great time, then they will tell their friends and invite them to the next one. You can do your own word of mouth publicity in the library. "Take Time to Talk to Your Librarian" was a method I used to promote a program during the Teen Read Week theme "Take Time to Read." I posted a sign in the YA room that told teens it would be rewarding to Take Time to Talk to me. When a teen approached me and said anything at all, I gave them a flyer about the program, a TRW bookmark, and a piece of candy from a bag as a treat. I introduced myself if they didn't already know me, invited them to the program, and answered any questions they had about it. The word spread that I was passing out candy, and I got to tell a lot of teens about the program. The teens enjoyed it and I was able to do some one-on-one promotion of the program and of my services. This idea could work for promoting any of your programs and gets you a lot of smiles from the teens in your library. Simple activities like this are inexpensive, fun, and make you more approachable.

Media

Newspapers, radio, and cable TV are all classic avenues for publicity and shouldn't be abandoned, but realize it may not reach the audience you are seeking first hand. Teachers and parents could forward the information to the students but sometimes that can backfire! If a program sounds like a good idea to your teacher or mom, how fun could it be?! Posting the newspaper articles on the bulletin board by a poster announcement for a program will help make the connection that the programs are also publicized in the newspaper. Some radio stations may allow teens to come in and record public service announcements. The other methods previously mentioned have the advantage of being free and you have a bit more control over the message. There's nothing worse for a program planner than reading an article about an upcoming program in the paper and seeing the wrong date!

Community Events

Our community has an annual Festival of Trees. The public is invited to tour the trees on the weekends between Thanksgiving and Christmas and vote for their favorites. The library has entered a tree for several years. The Friends of the Library sponsor the tree, buying any materials needed, and the TAB comes up with a theme and does the decorating. This event doesn't promote specific programs, but it is good publicity for the library and the TAB. The teens enjoy doing the project.

We have had a "Read When It Snows" tree with snowmen and snowflakes, a "Grinch Tree" that coincided with the release of the movie "How the Grinch Stole Christmas," and most recently "The Book Tree," which attracted a lot of attention on my Web site. A photo of "The Book Tree" was published in the January 2002 issue of *American Libraries*, which was a thrill to the teens (and me). I posted the photo on the YA bulletin board and had five new teens show up at the next TAB meeting!

Figure 14–6 The Book Tree.
The Book Tree was suggested at a TAB meeting. After some cre-ative engineering, a plan was drawn up and the teens constructed the tree in about an hour.

We will be participating in another festival in the fall. It is similar to the festival of trees, but it features scarecrows. We will be creating a scarecrow to represent the library. What local festivals and competitions are offered in your community? A parade float or a book cart drill team would attract attention to the great things happening in your library for teens. These are opportuni-ties for your teens to work on a project together, establishing long-time friend-ships. The teens will tell their friends and so on, and so on. . . .

RESOURCES

Honnold, RoseMary. *Hot Off the Press! Easy Steps to Publishing a Newsletter (with Teens!)* [Online]. Available: www.cplrmh.com/newsletter.html [2002, May 12].

McCracken, Linda D., and Lynne Zeiher. 2002. *The Library Book Cart Precision Drill Team Manual.* Jefferson, North Carolina: McFarland & Company.

Chapter 15

Record Keeping

OVERVIEW

Keeping good records of your programs is helpful in several ways. The numbers are important to your director and library board, so documenting attendance, participation, and expenses are essential to validate providing more programs. Other details are important to record as you review a program and think about what worked and what may need to be changed, improved, or abandoned. The time of year, day of the week, and time of day the program occurred are important to note as timing can affect attendance. The expense is not only important to document for the director, but also for your records as you plan for a year of programming on a limited budget. Details about contacts, supplies, sources, and books used will save time if you decide to repeat the program. Record what kind of publicity was done for the program and consider if it was enough or the right kind for that program. Also take time to think about what you would like to try next time and make notes of those ideas.

Program Records

All departments in our library write program records for the director. I keep a copy of every independent and social program record I do in a notebook in chronological order. I can look back through the year as I write my monthly and annual reports. I can also refer to the previous year's records when planning new programs. They have also been useful records for sharing with other librarians in presentations, building the *See YA Around* Web site and writing this book.

Program Title:	Countdown to Christmas Comics Giveaway
Program Intended For:	Grades 7-12
Date:	December 1-24, 2000
Time:	All open hours
Brief Description:	Teens entered to win a gift bag of comics-related items: comic books, posters, collector cards, and bookmarks. A winner was drawn every day.
Promotion:	E-mail newsletter, poster, and entry box in YA room, sign by front door.
Special Materials Required:	Prize items were collected from Naier and workshops
Costs:	Bookmarks and a poster were purchased from ALA to promote comics and graphic novels during the month of December.
Number of People:	260 entries, 24 winners
Staff Members Involved:	RoseMary Honnold
Evaluation and Comments:	Great response! Now I have to collect something else cheap to give away next December that will promote a collection . . . that's the problem with good ideas!

Figure 15–1 Program Record.
Keep records of all your programs. The information is helpful for planning new programs, writing annual reports, and for sharing with other librarians.

Evaluations

Evaluations give helpful feedback from participants and staff that helped during the program. When I held the first Science Fair Help Day, I gave each display table a yellow tablet and asked the participants to make any notes of additions or changes that we could do to make the next Help Day better. I received lots of positive reinforcement for the program and several ideas that we have added over the years. Add your own observations on the record form soon after a program while your memory is fresh.

I have also asked the Teen Advisory Board to make notes about the programs to give me their impressions and ideas for improvements or changes. I type up a list of the year's programs and pass copies out at a fall meeting and ask for feedback. They do not have to sign their names, so they can be honest. Listening to them discuss the different programs as they fill out this evaluation form is also insightful. A short report given at the TAB meeting about the last program will give the teens feedback for their involvement in the planning and implementation of the event. Ask the teens that attended what went well? What needs improvement for the next time?

Circulation Statistics

Take notice of any increase in circulation of materials related to your program topics and make a note of it in your program record for your director. A program can spark interest in a topic and you could discover your collection needs expansion or updating in those areas. Always have materials available for checkout at your social programs and book displays relevant to the independent programs in the YA room.

IS IT ALL ABOUT NUMBERS?

Circulation, attendance, expenses . . . all these numbers are easy to measure and compare. It sometimes seems that numbers are the only measure of success our supervisors or directors can see. There are some very important questions to ask yourself after a program. First, did the teens who attended have a good time? Did they ask when are you having the program again? Did they say thank you? These are the real measures of a successful program and the teens' reactions should be included in the report to the director.

A Final Word

My first goal in writing this book was to help young adult librarians build a strong, positive philosophy towards programming for teens based on the Developmental Assets suggested by The Search Institute. I believe the programs described in this book help teens build those assets by giving them opportunities for positive interactions and experiences at the library. Small libraries can have an active teen program and may actually get to build fuller relationships with the smaller audience of teens they serve. The quality of good teen programs and the positive attitude of the staff interacting with the teens will make positive contributions to the community and to individual lives.

Take some time to think of the adults that were important to you when you were a teen. What were the qualities they exhibited that impressed you? Good teen leaders are guides who respect teens, keep a sense of humor, and allow teens to explore and discover and create. Programming gives you an opportunity to build relationships with teens that may not have time to happen during the busy desk shifts.

Most of all, have fun with your job as a teen advocate in your library. Your positive attitude will influence the rest of the staff to react more positively with teens and invite positive feedback from the teens. If teens are 25 percent of our patrons, that will make 25 percent of everyone's jobs that much better!

Index of 101+ Programs

American Women Writers, 49
Animal Symbols, 49
Anthropology for Christmas, 129–130

Back to School Countdown, 47
Banned Books, 49
Beach Party Crafts, 124–126
Beach Party Games, 124–126
Beach Party Lock-In, 123–126
Beads! Beads! Beads!, 56–58
Board Game Nights, 91
Body in the Book Drop, 48
Book Terms, 49
Bookmark Contest, 52
Borders Shopping Trip, 157–160

Candle Making, 68–69
Carnival, 156
Chess Tournament, 91
Christmas Carry-In Dinner, 128–129
College Knowledge, 146–148
Composition, 99
Count the Peanuts, Jelly Beans, Candy
    Corn, etc., 47
Countdown to Christmas Comics
    Giveaway, 48
Cryptograms, Crosswords, and Other
    Games, 50

Dictionary Game, 133

Essay Contest, 52

Field Trips, 160

Halloween Decorating Party, 130
Holiday Trivia Quiz, 45–46
Human Bingo, 132

I Spy, 47
Independent Scavenger Hunt, 118–119
International Game Night, 149
Inventors Hall of Fame, 45
It's a Love Match, 43

Journal Making, 70–71
Just Another Love Song, 43

Library Survivor Scavenger Hunt, 112–
    117
Library Tour Scavenger Hunt, 118
Library Trivia, 46
Live Clue, 75–81

Mad Libs, 98–99
Mardi Gras Masks, 71
Medieval Festival, 153
Medieval Lock-In, 122
Mehndi Tattoo and a Taste of India,
    58–62
Misheard Lyrics, 44

Monopoly Tournament, 89–91
Mummy Wrap, 130–131
Music Revue/Karaoke, 99–102

Name That Poet, 43, 96–97
Name That Tune, 134
Newsletter Publication, 170–172

Open Mike Night, 102

Photography Contest, 52
Pizza Taste-Off, 126
Play-Doh Scupltionary, 134
Play To Win, 44
Poem Puzzle, 99
Poetry Board, 50, 96
Poetry Contest, 52
Poetry Machine, 98
Poetry Night, 93–99
Poster Contest, 52
Purchased Mystery Games, 75

Reader's Theater, 151–153
Religious Texts, 49
Role-Playing Games, 73–75

Sand Art, 62–63
Sand Painting, 63
Sardines, 133
Say What?, 49
Science Fair Help Day, 137–146
Scrabble Tournaments, 91
Scrapbook Picture Frames, 69–70
Shakespeare Glossary, 49
Soaps and Lotions/Aromatherapy, 66–
67
Songs Inspired by Literature, 44
Space Theme Lock-In, 122
Sports Team Trivia, 46
Sweet Heart Chat, 134
Summer Reading Program Circus
Theme, 28–31
Summer Reading Program History/
Medieval Theme, 36–37

Summer Reading Program International
Theme, 32–33
Summer Reading Program Ohio
Bicentennial Theme, 38
Summer Reading Program Space
Theme, 34–35
Survive Jeopardy and Feel Like a
Millionaire, 82–87

Teen Advisory Board, 166–168
Thesaurically Speaking, 49
Tie Dye, 64–66
Turkey Test, 46
TV Match Game, 44
TV Trivia and Other Trivia Games, 46
Twenty Questions, 134

Unmask the Athletes, 43
Unmask the Authors, 43
Unmask the Celebrities for Halloween,
42–43
Unmask the Celebrities for Mardi Gras,
42–43
Unmask the Musicians, 43
Unmask the Politicians, 43
Unmask the Winners, 43

Virtual Makeover Day, 51
Volunteens, 163–166

WDIM? (What Does It Mean?), 50
We Have a Mission! Scavenger Hunt,
106–111
What's so Great About Her?, 45
Which Century Was It?, 49
Who Makes That?, 45
Who Said That?, 44
Who Sells That??, 44
Who Wrote That??, 44
Who's Clowning Around?, 43
Whose Line Is It Anyway?, 88
Word Scrambles-Magazine ReQuest,
50
Word Trivia, 50

Index

A

Adolescent development, 1–3
ALA Celebrity READ posters, 99, 102
Alsdurf, Mamie, 10
American Library Association (ALA), 1, 19
Anthropology Game: In the Year 20001, 129–130
Application, college, 148
Application, Teen Advisory Board, 168
Aromatherapy, 66
Asimov, Isaac, 13
Assets, 1–3, 7–10
"At-risk" behavior, 3
Azadi, Javad, 92

B

Back to School Countdown, 47
Baker, Dustin, 92
Basic Metallurgy (Brown), 107
Bauer, Caroline Feller, 151
Beach Ball Volleyball, 124
Beach Blanket Bingo, 124–125
Beach Party Lock-In, 112–117
Beach party theme, 123–126
Beads! Beads! Beads! craft program, 56–58
Bindi, 60
Bingo, 124–125, 132–133
Board games, 89–91, 92
Body in the Book Drop game, 48

Bookmarks, 52
Book rating forms
    for circus theme, 29
    for history/medieval theme, 36
    for international theme, 32
    for space theme, 34
    for summer reading program, 25–26
Book-related games, 48–49
Book Tree, 176
Borders Shopping Trip, 157–160
Boundaries, 2, 8
Brown, Donald V., 107
Browning, Elizabeth Barrett, 99

C

Calendar, 19–23
Campus tours Web sites, 147
Candle making craft program, 68
Candy making craft program, 68–69
Carnival program, 156
Castle Clue, 76–81, 122
Chase's Calendar of Events (Whiteley), 41
Chess, 91
Children. *See* teens and children programs
Chocolate, 68–69
Christmas carry-in dinner, 128–129
Circulation statistics, 181
Circus theme, summer reading program, 28–31
Clipboard interview, 15

Clue, board game, 75
Coconut bowling, 125
Coffeehouse programs, 93–103
    collection connection, 102
    costs of, 102
    group poetry games, 98–99
    music review/karaoke, 99–102
    open mike night, 102
    poetry night, 93–98
    resources for, 103
    teen feedback on, 102–103
Collection connection
    for bead program, 58
    for board games, 91
    for coffeehouse programs, 102
    for College Knowledge, 149
    for independent programs/contests,
        53
    for lock-ins/holiday parties, 135
    for mehndi tattoo and Taste of India
        program, 62
    for role-playing games, 81
    for Sand Art/Sand Painting program,
        64
    for Science Fair Help Day, 146
    for soaps, lotions, aromatherapy, 67
    for summer reading programs, 38
    promotion of, 24
College Knowledge, 146–149
Commemorative occasions theme, 38
Community events, 175–176
Composition exercise, 99
Connecting Young Adults and Libraries
    (Jones), 1
Contests, 51–53
Coshocton Public Library
    permission slip of, 158
    scavenger hunts at, 105, 106–111
    summer reading program survey, 27
    Teen Advisory Board application,
        168
    year of YA programs, 19–23
Cosmopolitan Virtual Makeover 3.5, 51
Costs
    of board games, 91

of Borders Shopping Trip, 160
of coffeehouse programs, 102
of College Knowledge program, 148
of field trips, 160
of game programs, 91
of independent programs, 52–53
of International Game Night, 149–
    150
of lock-ins/holiday parties, 134–135
of mehndi tattoo and Taste of India
    program, 62
of Monopoly, Tournament, 90–91
of programs, 23
of role-playing games, 81
of Sand Art/Sand Painting program,
    63–64
of scavenger hunts, 119
of Science Fair Help Day, 146
of soaps, lotions, aromatherapy
    making, 67
of summer reading programs, 38
of teens and children programs, 153,
    156
of Tie Dye program, 66
record keeping and, 179
Couch Potato TV Trivia questions, 83
Countdown to Christmas Comics
    Giveaway, 48
Craft programs, 55–72
    Beads! Beads! Beads!, 56–58
    candle making, 68
    candy making, 68–69
    in general, 55
    journal making, 70–71
    Mardi Gras masks, 71
    mehndi Tattoo and Taste of India,
        58–62
    resources for, 71–72
    Sand Art and Sand Painting, 62–64
    scrapbook picture frames, 69–70
    soaps, lotions/aromatherapy, 66–67
    teen feedback on, 71
    Tie Dye, 64–66
Crosswords, 50
Cryptograms, 50

Cuyahoga County Public Library, 70

D

Development assets, 1–3
Dewey Decimal brainstorm, 19–23
Dewitt Wallace Fund, 1, 3
Dharma Trading Company, 64, 66
Dictionary game, 133
Display case, 173–174
Displays
    for bead programs, 56
    for Science Fair Help Day, 137–140,
        141
    for summer reading programs, 25
Dungeons and Dragons night, 74–75

E

E-mail list, 169–170
Empowerment, 2, 8
Essay contest, 52
Evaluations, 180–181
Expectations, 2, 8
Expenses. *See* costs
External assets, 2, 8–9

F

Feed the Dragon game, 153
Festival of Trees, 175
Field trips, 157–161
First Aid, 113
Fishing books, 114
Fish in the Moat game, 153
Flower Factory, 67
Food
    Christmas carry-in dinner, 128–129
    for beach party, 126
    for International Game Night, 149
    for lock-ins, 122
    for Medieval Fair, 155
    for poetry night, 97
    for teen programs, 11, 12
    party food ideas, 128
    pizza taste-off, 126–128
Friends group, 11
Frost, Robert, 98

G

Game programs
    board games, 89–91
    game show programs, 82–88
    International Game Night, 149–150
    resources for, 92
    role-playing games, 73–81
    teen feedback on, 91–92
Garcia, Marc, 92
Giveaway drawings, 48
Google, 42
Grass skirt hula contest, 125
Group poetry games, 98–99
Guessing games, 47–48

H

Halloween Decorating Party, 130
Hasbro, 89, 90
Haynes, Cathy, 48
Henna tattoos, 58–60
Herrage, Bonnie, 70
History/medieval theme, summer
    reading program, 36–37
Holiday parties, 128–130
Holiday trivia quiz, 45–46
Honnold, RoseMary, 4
Hook, Mellonee, 160
"How Do I Love Thee?" (Browning),
    99
Hula hoop contest, 125
Human Bingo, 132–133

I

Identity, positive, 2, 9
Independent programs and contests,
    41–54
    book-related games, 48–49
    collection connection, 53
    contests, 51–53
    giveaway drawings, 48
    guessing games, 47–48
    in general, 41–42
    matching games, 42–45
    resources for, 53–54
    trivia games, 45–46

virtual makeover day, 51
word games, 49–51
Independent scavenger hunts, 118–119
Internal assets, 2, 9
International Game Night, 149–150
International theme, summer reading
   program, 31–33
Internet, 11
I Spy guessing game, 47
"It's a Love Match" game, 43–44

J

Jones, Alison, 135, 161
Jones, Diane, 139–140
Jones, Patrick, 1–4, 19
Journal making craft program, 70–71
Junior Pictionary, 133

K

Karaoke/music review, 99–102
King of the Hill Tournament, 91

L

Learning, commitment to, 2, 9
Leeseberg, Ron, 138–139
Lei making, 124
Let's Get Ready to Rumble Sports Trivia
   questions, 84
Let's Make a Date game, 88
Librarianship, 10, 167
Library
   Borders Shopping Trip for, 157–160
   programs suited to, 14–19
   teen programming and, 7–12
   youth services of, 1, 3
Library Survivor scavenger hunt, 105,
   112–117, 119
Library Tour scavenger hunt, 105, 118,
   119
Library Trivia, 46
Literature Teacher's Book of Lists, The
   (Strouf), 41, 48
Live Clue, 75–81, 122
Lock-ins/holiday parties, 121–136
   Anthropology Game: In the Year

20001, 129–130
basic lock-in plan, 121–122
beach party theme, 123–126
Christmas carry-in dinner, 128–129
collection connection, 135
costs for, 134–135
Halloween Decorating Party, 130
Human Bingo, 132–133
medieval theme, 122
Mummy Wrap, 130–131
party food ideas, 128
pizza taste-off, 126–128
resources for, 136
space theme, 122
teen feedback on, 135–136
variations for, 133–134
Lotion making, 66
Lowe, Margaret, 138

M

Mad Libs, 98–99, 133
Mad Scientist Lab
   described, 139–140, 141
   experiment instructions, 143–146
   photo of, 142
Mandalas, 63
Mardi Gras masks, 71
Marvin, Sandy, 105, 119
Matching games, 42–45
McKinney, Roger, 154–155
Media, 175
Medieval Festival program, 153–155
Medieval theme, lock-ins, 122
Mehndi Tattoo and Taste of India craft
   program, 58–62
Mesaros, Sara, 140
Microscope, 146
Mid Ohio Library Organization
   (MOLO) YA Special Interest Group,
   18
Mini Putt Putt, 125
Misheard lyrics game, 44
Monopoly, Tournament, 89–91
Moore, Joel, 137
MS Publisher, 171

Mummy Wrap, 130–131
Music
    clipboard interview for, 15
    for poetry night, 95
    Name That Tune, 134
    review/karaoke, 99–102
Mystery games, 75, 81

N

Naeir, 11, 32, 48
Name That Poet game, 96, 97
Name That Tune game, 87, 134
Navajo Indians, 63
Newsletters, 170–172
Newspaper, 175

O

O Brother! Where Art Thou? (movie),
    106
O, Librarian! Where Art Thou: A
    Library Odyssey, 106
Online summer reading programs, 28
Open mike night, 102
Oriental Trading Company, 71
"Out of This World and into Books"
    reading theme, 34–35

P

Parents. *See* teens/parents programs
Party food ideas, 128
Patrons, 10
People Magazine, 43
Permission slip, 121, 158
Photography, 52
Photo release form, 173
Pizza taste-off, 126–128
Play-Doh Sculptionary, 134
Play to win game, 44
Poe, Edgar Allen, 98
Poem Puzzle, 99
Poetry board, 50–51, 96
Poetry contest, 52
Poetry games, group, 98–99
Poetry Machine, 98
Poetry night, 93–98

Pollcaster Web site, 28
Positive identity, 9
Positive values, 2, 9
Posters
    contest for, 52
    for circus theme, 31
    for poetry night, 93–94, 95, 96
*Presenting Reader's Theater: Plays and
    Poems to Read Aloud* (Bauer), 151
Prizes
    for beach party, 126
    for book rating forms, 25–26
    for contests, 51–52
    for game show programs, 82, 88
    for independent programs, 41–42,
        52–53
    for lock-ins, 122
    for scavenger hunts, 119
    for summer reading programs, 38
Program ideas, 13, 19–23, 55
Program planning
    collection connection, 24
    finding ideas, 19–23
    in general, 13–14
    resources for, 24
    scavenger hunts, 106
    teen feedback, 24
    that work in your library, 14–19
    time/costs for, 23
Program research, 14–19
Programs. *See* specific program names
*Programs for School-Age Youth in Public
    Libraries*, 1
Publicity, 169–177
    by word of mouth, 175
    community events for, 175–176
    display case for, 173–174
    e-mail list for, 169–170
    media for, 175
    newsletters for, 170–172
    resources for, 177
    schools for, 174
    survey and, 15
*"Public Libraries as Partners in Youth
    Development: Challenges and*

Opportunities""(Dewitt Wallace Fund), 3
Public relations, 140–141
Puzzlemaker Web site, 50
Puzzles
    for circus theme, 30
    for history/medieval theme, 37
    for international theme, 33
    for space theme, 35
    for summer reading program, 26

Q

Questions Only game, 88
Quia.com, 28

R

"The Raven" (Poe), 98
Reader's Theater program, 151–153
Reading Rocks Music Revue, 99–102
Record keeping, 179–181
    circulation statistics, 181
    evaluations, 180–181
    program records, 179–180
Research skills, 105–106
Resources
    for coffeehouse programs, 103
    for craft programs, 71–72
    for game programs, 92
    for independent programs and
        contests, 53–54
    for lock-ins/holiday parties, 136
    for planning programs, 24
    for publicity, 177
    for summer reading programs, 38–
        39
    for teens and children programs, 156
    for teens and parents programs, 150
Rewards, 166. *See also* prizes
Richcreek, Adam, 92
Ring the Flamingo's Neck, 126
"The Road Not Taken" (Frost), 98
Role Playing Club, 74, 91–92
Role-playing games, 73–81
    costs of, 81
    for collection connection, 81

    in general, 73–75
    Live Clue, 75–81
    mystery games, 75

S

Sand art, 124
Sand Art/Sand Painting craft program,
    62–64
Sand candles, 68
Sardines, 133–134
Say What? game, 49–50
Scavenger hunts, 105–119
    costs of, 119
    independent, 118–119
    in general, 105–106
    Library Survivor, 112–117
    Library Tour, 118
    We Have a Mission! Space Theme
        Scavenger Hunt, 106–111
Schedule, program, 23
Schlegel, Amy, 102, 135, 150, 160
Schools, 174
Science Fair Help Day, 137–146
Scrabble, 91
Scrapbook picture frames craft program,
    69–70
Search Institute, 1–3, 7–8
Sea shell mancala, 125
    See YA Around Web site, 179
Sheperd, Aaron, 152
Shroyer, Matt, 92, 135
SIBL Project, 44
Site-Seeing Tour for College Bound
    Students handout, 146, 147, 148
Soap craft program, 66–67
Social interaction, 8–9
Social programs, 28
Society for Creative Anachronisms, 154
Songs Inspired By Literature, 44
Space theme, lock-ins, 122
Space Theme Scavenger Hunt, We Have
    a Mission!, 105, 106–111, 119
Space theme, summer reading program,
    34–35
Spoons, 122

Sport Team Trivia, 46
Strouf, Judie L.H., 41, 48
Suggestion box, 14
Summer reading programs, 25–39
  basic, 25–28
  circus theme, 28–31
  collection connection and, 38
  commemorative occasions theme, 38
  costs of, 38
  history/medieval theme, 36–37
  international theme, 31–33
  lock-in party and, 121
  resources for, 38–39
  space theme, 34–35
Summer Reading Survey, 15
support, 2, 8
Surfing the Net With Kids Trivia Web
  site, 46
Surveys, 14–17, 27
Survive Jeopardy and Feel Like a
  Millionaire program, 82–87
Sweet Heart Chat, 134
Sweitzer, Andrea, 135, 156, 160

T
TAB. *See* Teen Advisory Board (TAB)
Take Time to Read Trivia questions, 84
"Take Time to Talk to Your Librarian"
  method, 175
Taste of India Meal, 61–62
Tattoos, 58–60
Teachers, 141
Teen Advisory Board (TAB)
  Borders Shopping Trip and, 157
  display case and, 173
  evaluations from, 180–181
  game ideas from, 73
  meeting times for, 23
  newsletters and, 170–171
  organizing, 166–168
  program poll, 15, 17
  teen programming and, 8
Teen Advisory Groups-Advisory
  Discussion (TAGAD-L), 167
Teen feedback

inclusion of, 24
  on board games, 91–92
  on coffeehouse programs, 102–103
  on craft programs, 71
  on field trips, 160–161
  on game programs, 91–92
  on lock-ins/holiday parties, 135–136
  on Science Fair Help Day, 150
  on teens and children programs, 156
Teen magazines, 18
Teen programming, 7–12
  benefits for library, 10
  benefits for teens, 7–10
  funds for, 11–12
Teen Read Week survey, 15, 16
Teens and children programs, 151–156
  Carnival, 156
  Medieval Festival, 153–155
  Reader's Theater, 151–153
  resources for, 156
  teen feedback on, 156
Teens/parents programs, 137–150
  College Knowledge, 146–149
  International Game Night, 149–150
  Science Fair Help Day, 137–146
Teen volunteer programs, 163–168
  good volunteers, tips for, 165–166
  in general, 163–164
  jobs for, 164–165
  rewards for, 166
  Teen Advisory Board, organizing,
    166–168
Test prep web sites, 147
Thesaurically Speaking game, 49
Tie Dye craft program, 64–66
Time, use of, 2, 8–9
Trick or Treat Halloween Trivia
  questions, 86
Trivia games, 45–46, 82–87
Turkey Test, 46
TV Trivia, 46
Twenty Questions, 134
Two Thumbs Up Movie Trivia ques-
  tions, 85

U

Unmask the Celebrities game, 42–43
Unmask the Musicians game, 102
Urban Libraries Council, 3

V

Values, positive, 2, 9
Virtual makeover day, 51
Volunteen group, 163
Volunteer programs. *See* teen volunteer
   programs

W

Walters, Travis, 135–136, 156, 161
Want Fries With That? Trivia questions,
   85
Warhammer, 73, 74–75
WDIM? *See* What Does It Mean game

We Have a Mission! Space Theme
   Scavenger Hunt, 105, 106–111, 119
What Does It Mean? (WDIM?) game,
   50
"What's so Great About Her?" game,
   45
"Where in the World Are You Read-
   ing?" theme, 32–33
Whiteley, Sandy, 41
Whose Line Is It Anyway? game, 88
Word games, 49–51
Word of mouth, 175
Word scrambles, 50
Word trivia, 50

Y

Young, Shaleen, 71
"Your Library: The Greatest Show in
   Town" theme, 28–31

About the Author

RoseMary Honnold is the young adult librarian coordinator at the Coshocton Public Library. She and her husband, Mike, have survived raising two terrific daughters, caring for several foster children, and hosting a few exchange students. Her family has expanded to include two wonderful sons-in-law and an active, entertaining grandson. Taking classes and teaching Sunday school are other activities she finds time to do. Free time is spent reading, painting in acrylic and watercolor, and thinking up teen programs. RoseMary has a painting gallery online at www.geocities.com/rhonnold.

The creator of the *See YA Around* Web site has written for *VOYA* and YALSA's online newsletter and spoken at several conferences and workshops about teen programming. *101+ Teen Programs That Work* is her first book.